PARROTS

'We humans have tended to cast the parrot in the role of the over-painted, loud-mouthed clown, but the part is unworthy of the actor. In real life, parrots are masterpieces of animal design, whose private lives are full of fascination and, in many cases, mystery.'

PARROTS
A Natural History

JOHN SPARKS

with

TONY SOPER

Illustrated by Robert Gillmor

Facts On File
New York • Oxford • Sydney

FOR SARA

Facts On File, Inc.
460 Park Avenue South
New York NY 10016
USA

Library of Congress Cataloguing-in-Publication Data

Sparks, John
    1. Parrots: a natural history/by John Sparks.
    Includes bibliographical references.
    ISBN 0-8160-2427-8
    1. Parrots. I. Title.
QL696.P7S63   1990
598'.71--dc20   89-48332
                                                      CIP

Facts On File books are available at special discounts when
purchased in bulk quantities for businesses, associations,
institutions or sales promotions. Please contact the
Special Sales Department of our New York office at
212/683-2244 (dial 800/322-8755 except in NY, AK or HI).

Printed in Great Britain

10 9 8 7 6 5 4 3 2 1

CONTENTS

Pollybirdia Singularis
(Edward Lear)

INTRODUCTION
by Tony Soper

There is nothing subtle about parrots. Everything about them seems to be designed for showing off. They are the original op-art posters, advertising themselves with vivid, saturated colours applied with scant regard for composition. Natural parrot talk, more often than not, is no more harmonious than their plumage; their voices rend the air with calico-tearing shrieks and squawks sufficient to shatter the eardrums. More than one pet parrot has been taken to court for disturbing the peace! On first acquaintance, parrots appear to be gawky, suffering the indignity of an outsize beak, and moving without the grace so characteristic of most other birds. In flight, parrots both great and small cleave the air with whirring, noisy wings; on the ground, they lurch from one foot to the other in a drunken waddle.

Nevertheless, parrots and their kin are undeniably endearing creatures. They jostle for our affections with other popular birds like owls and penguins. Indeed, parrots were one of the natural treasures brought back from the tropics as the borders of the known world were

7

expanded by European navigators and traders. Such was the impact that these singular birds made upon Portuguese and Spanish explorers venturing across uncharted oceans, that both South America and Australia were first referred to as 'the land of the parrot' and the 'region of parrots' respectively. However, along with the cutlass and eyepatch, a parrot became part of a uniform – no self-respecting buccaneer sailing under the Jolly Roger was without his tame macaw or amazon cursing and uttering foul oaths.

Here lies one of the parrot's great virtues; many of them are accomplished mimics, so giving them a head start over other birds in winning our admiration. At the drop of a peanut, a pet parrot can imitate with astonishing accuracy anything from the sound of a dripping tap to a particular human's voice. And whatever can speak may be suspected of a sense of humour. Thus, the talking parrot has become something of a music-hall joke, a blasphemer, a shocker of maiden ladies and prudish vicars and, above all, a mischief maker.

There was an old man of Dunrose;
A parrot seized hold of his nose.
When he grew melancholy, They said, 'His name's Polly,'
Which soothed that old man of Dunrose.

(Edward Lear)

Not without reason. During World War II, many a bird fancier was sent diving for cover by the whistle of falling bombs, only to be jeered by the cackle of a pet parrot!

In our eyes, the parrot has often taken on the role of a comedian licensed to take outrageous liberties. Even in Tudor times a 'popinjay' was considered a social asset and took its place alongside the jesters in all high-ranking courts. Today, ownership still confers status and these hugely expensive pets are avidly bred and collected by aviculturists the world over. This so-called 'parrot fever' has stoked a tremendous trade in these birds – part of it illegal – with rich profits; a single palm cockatoo smuggled out of South East Asia is reputed to fetch upward of $30,000 in the USA, a Spix's or Lear's macaw commands virtually whatever the seller chooses to ask for it. Unfortunately, this very popularity has placed the survival of several kinds of wild parrot in jeopardy. The pressure is something that they could do without, because, being fundamentally birds of the rain forest, their homes are already being destroyed at a frightening rate to provide timber and to make way for farming. These problems do not apply to the budgerigar, however. Breeding freely in captivity, the diminutive, baby-faced parrot is doing well as a human companion and is the most numerous pet bird today.

One of the first people to popularise parrots was Edward Lear, whose chief claim to fame was his Nonsense Rhymes. In fact he made some serious observations on these birds, and produced forty-one lithographs which were published between 1830 and 1832. In quality, they match the excellence of John James Audubon's art. John Gould, who liked to be known as 'The Bird Man' also produced a stunning portfolio of parrots for his outstanding work *The Birds of Australia*, thus helping to popularise the birds themselves yet further. Each of the 250 sets produced between 1840 and 1848 originally cost £115; today the plate of the Major Mitchell's cockatoo alone sells for £10,000. Whichever way you look at them, parrots are big business.

Our aim is more modest. It is not our purpose to present an exhaustive guide to the 333 or so species. Neither have we attempted to provide a text for serious aviculturists, because parrot keepers have been well provided with books about how to house and care for these birds.

Introduction

Parrots, A Natural History provides a broad account of this fascinating order of birds, collating between one set of covers the basic biology and the history of discovery of the Psittaciformes so that the family budgie or talking African grey parrot can be viewed in perspective against the group of birds in general.

We humans have tended to cast the parrot in the role of the over-painted, loud-mouthed clown, but the part is unworthy of the actor. In real life, parrots are masterpieces of animal design, whose private lives are full of fascination and, in many cases, mystery.

2 · PARROTS AS BIRDS

One could be forgiven for thinking that parrots are not 'real' birds. A pathetic polly shackled to a perch, or a budgie imprisoned in a cage with only its doting owner and a mirror for companionship hardly reveal that quintessential of avian properties – an ability to fly. Unfortunately, in the northern hemisphere, most of us are not well placed to watch wild parrots in action. However, fly they certainly do, because most of them are ace aeronauts. Indeed, their capacity for sustained, swift and powerful flight often makes them elusive quarry for naturalists. The smaller kinds, like the sharp-winged parakeets and lovebirds, are restless and always on the move. They cleave the air with whirring wings, speeding across forest canopies, and vanish from view before binoculars can be properly trained upon them. Many of the medium-sized parrots are no easier to observe, often exploding from the foliage with a flash of dazzling plumage, their screeches receding into the distance. Even the big macaws and cockatoos are buoyant fliers, revelling in their mastery of the air, swerving and swooping at speed as they go about their daily business.

11

PSITTACIFORMES

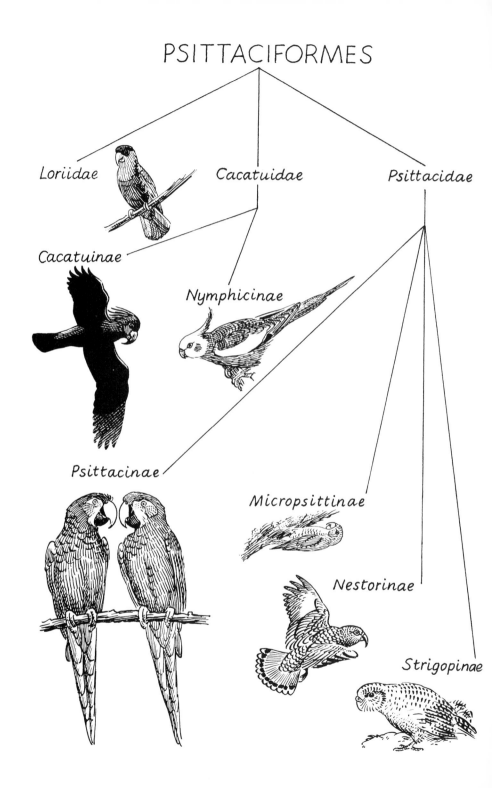

Loriidae

Cacatuidae

Psittacidae

Cacatuinae

Nymphicinae

Psittacinae

Micropsittinae

Nestorinae

Strigopinae

Of course, parrots are proper birds, and yet they are undeniably unique in many ways. They are the 'monkeys' of the bird world and betray their arboreal roots by the design of their bodies. As we shall see, they illustrate the principle that 'you are what you eat'! Most of them are no friend of plants because they are 'seed killers' and many of the features that distinguish them from other birds, like their massive decurved beaks, enable parrots to rob plants of their investment in future generations – their seed.

WHAT IS A PARROT?

There are 333 kinds of birds placed in the Psittaciformes, one of 29 great orders into which the bird kingdom is divided. They range in size from the metre-long hyacinth macaw to the tiny pygmy parrots from South East Asia, one of which could lie comfortably on the palm of your hand. Although they are a tightly knit group, we have given them a number of names that do not always reflect natural relationships within the family. The term 'parrot' is usually reserved for any small to medium-sized, stumpy-tailed bird. A variety of long-tailed species from Australasia, Africa and South America are often called 'parakeets', although in Australia this name is not used; down under, a parakeet is a 'parrot'. Some names do reflect natural groups; the 17 kinds of crested 'cockatoos' from Australasia are closely related to each other, as are the 17 species of macaws from South America. There are parrots called amazons, cockatiels, conures, caiques, lories, lorikeets, lorilets, lovebirds, parrotlets, rosellas, night parrots, and ground parrots; there is also a selection of unusual New Zealand species with Maori names – kaka, kakapo, and kea. And yet, despite this diversity of terms, there is no mistaking a parrot because they are all constructed along the same lines.

Every parrot is endowed with a great hooked beak, its downward curving upper mandible largely fitting over the smaller bottom one. Sitting astride the bill, the nostrils are set in an area of bare skin called the cere, which is particularly noticeable in the budgerigar where it is blue in the cocks and brown in the hens. Parrots are also distinguished by their yoke-toed feet and a tendency to possess green plumage.

These peculiarities are the outcome of the demands of making a living in the treetops. Many other birds spend their lives in the forest canopy, but parrots have been able to carve out a special niche for themselves, perhaps because they are rather more adept than most birds in climbing like acrobats. They achieve this by the skilful coordination of grappling beak and grasping feet, a talent that enables parrots to reach the outermost flimsy branches of trees with the minimum of effort when compared with flying and hovering. Once they are out on a limb, they are able to plunder the rich harvest of flowers, fruits and seeds beyond the reach of many creatures of their size.

Admittedly, many parrots have broken the link with their woodland origins, especially in Australia. However, even those kinds that live in arid grasslands or high in mountains beyond the tree-line retain the anatomical legacy that evolved in the swaying green vaults of their ancestral home.

WHERE DO PARROTS LIVE?

Parrots are basically birds of tropical and sub-tropical forests, and chiefly confined to the southern hemisphere. However, less than a hundred years ago, people who lived in the south and east of the USA would have seen flocks of Carolina parakeets, the most northerly representatives of the family in historical times. James Audubon, the celebrated American artist, shot some parakeets and recorded their images for posterity in one of his magnificent lithographs. Alas, the species became officially extinct in 1914. Nowadays, the slaty-headed parakeet takes credit for being the most northerly native parrot as it occurs naturally in eastern Afghanistan at 34 degrees north. However, some species have been introduced by man into even more northern climes where they are surviving happily. For instance, Monk parakeets from Brazil and central Argentina are established around New York and northern New Jersey. Even rose-ringed parakeets, a particularly widespread species, have become permanently established in south-east England. They originated from escaped cage birds, although some may have been deliberately released.

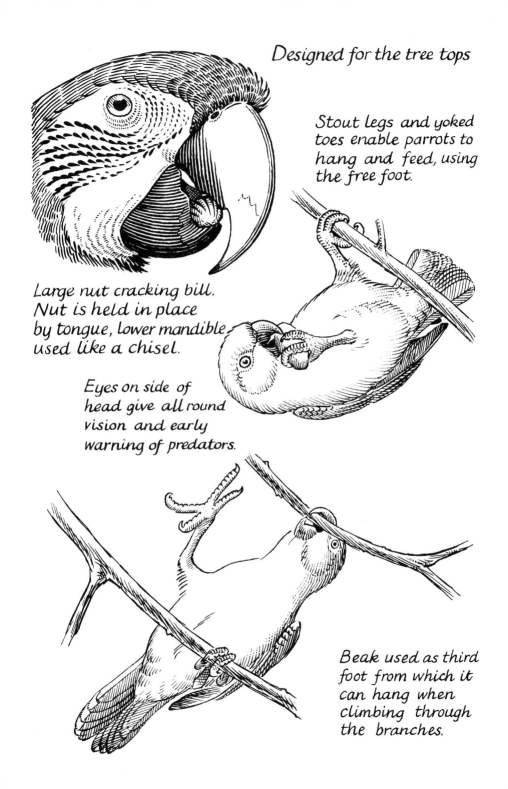

Designed for the tree tops

Stout legs and yoked toes enable parrots to hang and feed, using the free foot.

Large nut cracking bill. Nut is held in place by tongue, lower mandible used like a chisel.

Eyes on side of head give all round vision and early warning of predators.

Beak used as third foot from which it can hang when climbing through the branches.

The most southerly members of the family are the Austral conure and the red-fronted parakeet. The former is moss green and lives in the austere southern beech forests of Chile and Argentina up to 55 degrees south, while the latter species used to eke out a living among the bleak, wind-swept tussock grass of Macquarie Island well within the limit of Antarctic ice-floes. Unfortunately, this species was exterminated by cats just before World War I, although other sub-species of these little green parakeets survive on other offshore refuges belonging to New Zealand. But on Antipodes Island, at 50 degrees south, it is still possible to see New Zealand's largest parakeet frequenting penguin rookeries where it scratches for flies and grubs among the guano, or fossicks along the tide-line between fur seals.

Pages 18–19: A variety of species of parrots *(Illustrated by Robert Gillmor)*

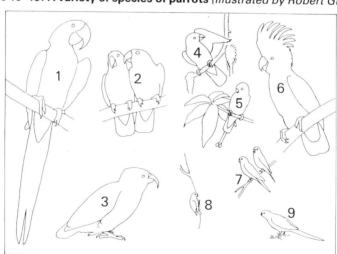

1 Hyacinth macaw *Anodorhynchus hyacinthinus,* 100cm (39½in), Brazil
2 Eclectus parrot *Eclectus roratus* (male on right), 35cm (13¾in), New Guinea, Australia
3 Kea *Nestor notabilis,* 48cm (19in), New Zealand
4 Black-capped lory *Lorius lory somu,* 31cm (12¼in), New Guinea
5 Mountain racket-tailed parrot *Prioniturus*
m. montanus, 30cm (11¾in), Philippines
6 Salmon-crested cockatoo *Cacatua moluccensis,* 52cm (20½in), Indonesia
7 Scarlet-chested parrot *Neophema splendida* (male on left), 19cm (7½), Australia
8 Buff-faced pygmy parrot *Micropsitta p. pusio,* 8.5cm (3⅜in), New Guinea
9 Ground parrot *Pezoporus w. wallicus,* 30cm (11¾in), Australia

Opposite: *A pair of hyacinth macaws, one preening the head of the other* (Kenneth W. Fink/ Photo Researchers Inc)

Although lush forest is the favoured home for most parrots, as a family they range over all kinds of countryside. There are, for example, distinctive highland forms such as the exquisite Papuan lory whose plumage and long tail streamers are much sought after by tribesmen for feather head-dresses. These parrots live in·the cool cloud forests which, up to an altitude of 3,500m (11,480ft), clothe the central mountains of Irian Jaya and Papua New Guinea. The Derbyan parakeet occurs in Tibet, and the yellow-faced parrot is found in the *Hagenia* and cedar-podocarp forests in the highlands of Ethiopia. Even snow is familiar to some parrots. Although Australia is largely a hot, flat continent, the southern mountains of the Great Divide regularly attract a covering of snow, and this is where the gang-gang occurs – a rather aberrant grey cockatoo with a scarlet hood surmounted by a few absurd curly feathers. Brilliantly coloured crimson rosellas also feed in areas of the Great Divide blanketed by winter snow, their blood-red plumage dramatically contrasting with the glaring white landscape. Across the Tasman Sea, kea, hefty green parrots, survive high above the snow line in the New Zealand Alps, often loafing around ski resorts where they thrive on scraps and vandalise anything that they can get their powerful beaks around. There are even parrots that live on the coast like seagulls. In Australia, the rather drab rock parrot inhabits cliffs and islands off the south and west coast, and numerous species have spread out into the sun-scorched centre, well away from their ancestral forested areas. For example, budgerigars are at home in the arid parts of central Australia, and can even survive without water for several weeks providing they can feed on moist food.

THE ORIGIN OF PARROTS

No one knows for sure when parrots first appeared on this planet. It is not even very easy to determine with any degree of certainty to what other kinds of birds they are most closely related. The fossil record is no help except to establish the fact that they are a very ancient family

John Gould's lithograph of a pair of Major Mitchell's cockatoos (by courtesy of the British Museum (Natural History))

Red-fronted Parakeets with Royal Penguins

indeed, and were perfectly good parrots by the time they first appeared in it.

Remains of forest birds do not readily preserve. Their bones are light and fragile and the chances are that they will become broken and the pieces dispersed before the processes of fossilization can get underway. However, ancient remains of parrots have been discovered although, curiously enough, not in Australia or South America. The oldest fossil parrot bone was discovered in Allier in France. It was a taro-metatarsus – a leg bone – and its age has been estimated at 30 million years. The bird from which it came has been named *Archaeopsittacus verreauxi* and, from the evidence, was a perfectly good parrot that would not have looked out of place today in the Amazon rainforest. Another fossil found in Nebraska, USA, was assessed at 20 million years old, and was placed in the same genus, *Conuropsis*, as the recently extinct Carolina parakeet. We can therefore conclude that parrots, as we largely know them, have been around for at least 30 million years, and so must have diverged from an ancestral stock maybe tens of millions of years previously.

Bird taxonomists have always tended towards the view that pigeons may be closer to parrots than any other group of birds. Both types possess a fleshy cere at the base of the beak, and share a taste for fruit and seeds, although the pigeon's strategy is to use a powerful gizzard to attack armoured seeds rather than a 'nutcracker' bill. Pigeons and some parrots also drink by drawing long draughts with the beak immersed, rather than by dipping and tilting the head backwards.

Recent, highly detailed analyses of DNA – the chemical that inherited genes are made of – has thrown a little new light onto the question of parrot relationships within the bird world. The method was pioneered by Professor Charles Sibley in the USA and is based upon the assumption that proteins change less swiftly than bodies; two animals may look quite different, but if the chemical properties of their DNA are similar, this indicates a fairly close relationship based upon common ancestry. Professor Sibley and his two colleagues, Jon Ahlquist and Burt Monroe Jr, have proposed a refined classification of birds based upon their work. It confirms the fact that parrots stand alone as a discrete group, that is, they are not very close to any particular group, thus verifying what we already knew about their long period of independence. However, the results revealed that parrot DNA shared certain characteristics with that of a number of other clusters of families including the swifts, trogons, owls and cuckoos. From this it seems that the link with pigeons may be more tenuous than was previously thought.

By looking at the geographical distribution of parrots, it is possible to say something about where parrots may have originated.

PARROT DISTRIBUTION

Parrots have a peculiar pattern of distribution. There are relatively few kinds in the northern hemisphere and none now live naturally (apart from introduced species) in North America, Europe or the USSR. Only 34 kinds occur in Africa, India and South East Asia. By far the largest concentration of species live in South and Central America, including Mexico. No less than 210 different kinds – or nearly two-thirds of all parrots – live in that sector of the planet; 70 have been recorded in Brazil alone. However, these New World parrots form a comparatively homogeneous collection of species when compared with the Australasian representatives. Although only 109 kinds of parrots live in Australasia, New Zealand and the Philippines, they are an astonishingly diverse group. It is as though the basic parrot design has been more thoroughly developed and exploited by the forces of evolution in the Antipodes. Could South America or Australia be the ancestral home of this great family of birds? The unusual distribution of parrots certainly needs some explanation.

It is tempting to argue that, being essentially pan-tropical birds, parrots are unable to tolerate cool climates, and so were unable to colonise the northern parts of the world. However, Carolina parakeets used to survive as far north as Wisconsin, which is on the same latitude as Madrid and Peking. Climate may not therefore have been an important impediment to the northward spread of these birds in Eurasia. Indeed, no less than seventy kinds of parrots occur below the Tropic of Capricorn where the weather is comparable to that found over much of southern Europe and Asia. Another theory for the southerly bias in the range of parrots is that the advance of the glaciers and tundra during the height of the last Ice Age caused parrots to retreat from much of the northern lands. When the ice retreated, the northern advance of parrots may have been blocked by such barriers as the Himalayas and both the Saharan and Arabian Deserts. This suggestion is supported by the fossil evidence that these birds lived in Europe well before the onset of the last Ice Age, but not afterwards. But there may be more to the story.

The range of parrots, and their adaptive radiation in Australia, has more than a passing similarity to that of the pouched or marsupial mammals like kangaroos and possums. It is therefore tempting to speculate that they might share the same roots in the great supercontinent of Gondwanaland. To understand this, it is necessary to consider the way in which the continents have waltzed around the globe and influenced the distribution of wildlife.

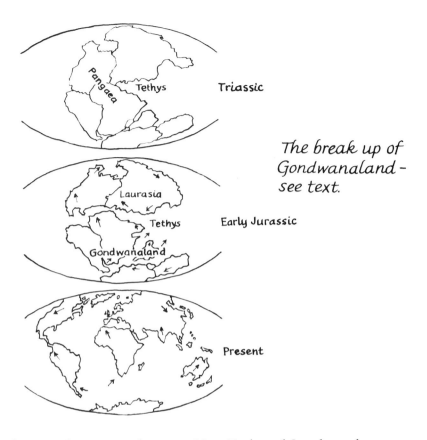

Triassic

Tethys

Pangaea

The break up of
Gondwanaland –
see text.

Laurasia

Tethys

Early Jurassic

Gondwanaland

Present

Each year, the journey between New York and London takes a fraction of a second longer because the Atlantic Ocean is spreading, forcing North America and Europe further apart. The reason is that the major land masses are 'floating' like rafts or plates on the fluid interior of our planet and are being shifted around by titanic convection forces beneath the crust. Where the plates grind against each other, earthquakes periodically shake the ground, volcanoes spew out molten larva, or mountain ranges rear up, sometimes buckling the sea bed and heaving it thousands of metres into the air. Although the atlas of the world appears to reflect a static planet, the fact is that the geography of the world is still in a state of flux. Down under, Australia is moving on a collision course with Asia at a breakneck speed of 7cm (2.7in) a year!

When the sun was beginning to set upon the Age of Dinosaurs, the southern hemisphere was dominated by the remnants of the already

25

mentioned land called Gondwana. Its surface was rippled here and there by mountains; forests of southern beech (*Nothofagus*), tree ferns and cycads covered its surface. Scurrying through the undergrowth were possum-like creatures which had developed the marsupial strategy of reproduction with brief pregnancies and the young spending a period from shortly after birth clamped to their mother's nipple, sometimes protected in a pouch. Monster flightless birds, some savage killers, plodded their way like cassowaries through those ancient woodlands, while other birds undoubtedly graced the skies; after all, flying birds had made an appearance in the pageant of life at least 60 million years previously. Then, about 65 million years ago, gigantic tension in the earth's mantle caused the final fragmentation of Gondwana. By then, vast pieces that were to become India and Africa had already rafted away to the north. Now, millimetre by millimetre, the mighty portion that was to become Australia drifted away, to be followed 25 million years later by the huge slice that we now call South America. What remained became frigid and glaciated and formed Antarctica.

Each of these continental rafts carried a complement of animals and plants like so many Noah's Arks. The first to go, India and Africa, ultimately came to rest against the underbelly of Eurasia; South America collided with North America to which it became joined by an isthmus. These all became colonised by life forms that evolved in the northern regions of the planet and to which many of the indigenous animals and plants succumbed. Australia was different. It remained an island – a lost world adrift beneath the Tropic of Capricorn – so largely preserving the integrity of its Gondwanan inheritance, at least until recently, and this accounts for its unusual marsupial fauna and many of its birds.

The choreography of these jostling continents explains some curiosities of plant and animal distribution. Alfred Russel Wallace, the Victorian naturalist, was one of the first to discover odd facts about animal geography when he was collecting specimens in the Malay Peninsula. In 1856, he was hoping to obtain a passage direct from Singapore to Macassar, but was forced to go to Bali and, from there, crossed the narrow but deep strait to Lombok. In doing so, he chanced upon the frontier between two great zoological divisions, based upon separate continental plates, which is still called Wallace's Line. To the west, Bali had all the characteristics of an Asian island, but to the east on Lombok there were, among other things, sulphur-crested cockatoos and mound building birds typical of Australia. There are many other anomalies.

Gloomy forests of the rather primitive southern beech are found in both Australia and South America; on the other hand, wonderfully resplendent Banksias decorate both the Australian and South African countryside. Among the mammals, marsupials are today confined only to Australia and South America, though the Virginian opossum has penetrated the USA across the Central American peninsula. However, Australia has by far the greatest diversity of these creatures. That is perhaps not surprising because the island continent was isolated for longer, allowing evolution to work its creative magic on the primitive Gondwanan castaways. South America was originally a marsupial stronghold, but was invaded from the north by several waves of 'higher' eutherian mammals such as primates, carnivores and hoofed mammals to which many marsupial types gave way. Today, only nocturnal opossums survive.

Parrots have a range consistent with the notion that they evolved somewhere in the Gondwanan province. Of course being birds, and strong flying ones at that, it is to be expected that they would have moved between adjacent land masses. However, with so many species centred upon Australia and South America, it seems likely that the ancestors of our modern parrots were predominant members of the community that inhabited the forests which covered the core of that ancient continent. The fossil evidence certainly supports the possibility because parrots are ancient birds indeed.

We can therefore conclude that parrots, as we largely know them, have been around for more than 30 million years and, from the way they have speciated in both Australia and South America, they could easily have their roots in that mysterious southern continent of Gondwanaland.

PRETTY POLLIES

Taken as a family, parrots have been described as living palettes of vivid primary colours. Admittedly some, such as the Seychelles black parrot of Praslin Island, rate among the dullest of birds; however, for most the striking feature is the brilliant nature of their plumage. Sometimes the saturated colours seem to have been applied with bold sweeps of a brush with little consideration for blending and composition, thus conferring upon these birds a kind of vulgarity. Nevertheless, the exuberance of colour is frequently a feast for the eye, and justifies the notion that they are carnival birds par excellence.

The family also includes some of the most beautiful birds in the world. The diminutive splendid parakeet (called the red-chested parrot in Australia) takes a lot of beating because it is a living prism, glinting with all the colours of the rainbow. The rich indigo of the head shades to a lovely jade green on the back. When the wings are unfurled, the front coverts flash the brightest azure imaginable. The belly is canary yellow, and attention is drawn to the chest by a dramatic splash of scarlet. Other parrots, such as the crimson rosella and the eclectus, have plumages which appear to have been fashioned out of plush red and green velvet. The eclectus was originally something of a mystery because the sexes are so different from each other that they were assigned to separate species, the cock being essentially green and the hen deep vermilion. The gorgeous king parrot, which visits lawns in the suburbs of Sydney, likewise has an intense scarlet body with luminous turquoise epaulettes. The sun conure from the northern Amazonian forests is well named because of its brilliant saffron plumage, washed here and there with orange to stunning effect – a real splash of golden sunshine.

Not all parrots are poster coloured. Major Mitchell's cockatoo – sometimes referred to as Leadbeater's – from the arid parts of western and southern Australia, is a delicate pink confection, with a startling flame-red flash concealed in its crest. The soft, subtle blend of pinks, Georgian green and violet of the princess parakeet is sympathetic to the shades found in central Australia where nomadic flocks live.

Many parrots are basically green, although the hues vary enormously from one species to another. The New Zealand kakapo could be mistaken for a lump of moss; others reflect the colours of jade, emerald and verdite. There are even sooty brown parrots, like the vasa parrot from Madagascar which looks like a dirty scrawny pigeon. Others vary in shade from khaki, through mahogany to iridescent bronze. A few parrots are black and grey, although their sombre coloration is usually relieved by dramatic patches of red or yellow.

When parrots are exhibited against unnatural backgrounds, they usually draw the eye. In those circumstances, they appear to have been the objects of evolutionary indulgence. And yet, in the wild many parrots are far from conspicuous. Indeed, the florid colours often help the birds to vanish from view. For example, small parties of multi-coloured rainbow lorikeets from Australia are far from easy to observe when feeding in the crowns of flowering eucalyptus trees. The plumage may be boldly patterned with blue, yellow and orange, but the green upper parts enable them to merge with the foliage when viewed from a distance. The fact is, greenish parrots tend to be camouflaged.

Colour matching is one of the chief principles of camouflage, and many parrots are masters of this technique. Animals which live for much of the time surrounded by green leaves are at an advantage if they are green, blue or yellow because these colours offer the best chance of concealment amidst foliage. Many arboreal creatures, both hunters and hunted, have independently evolved greenish coloration. Numerous groups of insectivorous birds like warblers, tits and white-eyes possess leaf-green livery. So do many pigeons, African touracos, South East Asian leaf birds and bulbuls, to mention but a few. Tree snakes of different kinds (eg pythons and mambas), chameleons, various lizards, and large numbers of insects and their larvae have all developed green colour schemes as part of their strategies for surviving in the canopy. Even dazzling yellow takes on a low-key greenish hue in the ambient light of a forest, as anyone who has tried to spot golden orioles at home in their leafy setting knows.

Splashes of vivid colour in the plumage of many parrots may also help to disrupt the bird's outlines. They deceive predators, leading their eyes away from the edge of the parrot's body. As hawks and falcons undoubtedly learn to recognise a square meal by the shape of the prey, any trick which hides the characteristic avian shape should have survival value. The bold patterns displayed by many kinds of plovers, and on the flanks of some gazelles, are examples of disruptive coloration. But, in the case of parrots, deceit is involved in the very generation of the colours themselves, because there is rather less to parrot coloration than meets the eye.

A bird which reflects all the daylight that falls on it will appear white – like the white cockatoo from the central and northern Moluccas. However, feathers which remove part of the spectrum of incident light appear coloured. This is achieved by two methods – pigments or trickery, or by a combination of both techniques. Many of the rich colours we perceive in the plumage of parrots are an illusion. Green, blue and plum coloured feathers contain no such pigments at all. Even the deep purple coloration of the hyacinth macaw is generated by a miraculous alchemy of light. The phenomenon of Tyndall scattering is responsible for the illusion, as it is for making the vault of the sky appear blue. When white light, which is a mixture of all the colours of the spectrum, passes through a suspension of exceedingly minute droplets or particles, the shorter wavelengths of light at the blue end of the spectrum are scattered back. In the atmosphere, dust and water particles cause the scattering, thereby giving the sky its blue colour. In the feathers of parrots, the job is done by countless millions of microscopic air vacuoles forming a 'cloudy' layer in the horny substance of the barbs. These are so small that the diameter of the bubbles is well below the wavelength of visible light. The Tyndall effect is reinforced by deposits of dark melanin granules which absorb light from the red end of the spectrum, leaving the blue alone to reflect back. Such feathers (eg those from the back of the blue and yellow macaw) appear brown when held up against the light, but immediately turn an azure blue in incident light.

'Parrot green' is produced with the help of a yellow pigment. This is laid down in the surface layers of the feathers and interacts with Tyndall blue to produce the illusion of green. If the yellow pigment is artificially removed by alcohol, the feathers turn blue. This occasionally happens in the wild through genetic mutation among budgerigars.

They are naturally green birds, but every now and again a blue 'sport' turns up. When such aberrantly coloured individuals were first secured by aviculturists just over half a century ago, they were greatly prized. Nowadays, strains of blue and cobalt birds are commonplace; indeed, blue 'sports' have arisen in several kinds of basically green parrots, including the black-faced lovebird and rose-ringed parakeet.

The iridescence displayed by the feathers of some parrots, eg a few of the amazons, is caused by yet another optical phenomenon called 'interference'; this is responsible for the sheen of oil on water that changes hue with the viewing angle. No colouring matter is involved. The structure of the feather surface simply reflects light in such a way that certain wavelengths are cancelled while others are reinforced, thus imparting a metallic blue or green veneer to the plumage.

There is another strange fact about parrot coloration. Some of them possess feathers which fluoresce yellow or green under ultraviolet light. This means that they would glow nicely in discos! The ability is due to a unique pigment found in no other birds. The yellow pigment in the plumage of green budgerigars glows in the dark when illuminated by ultraviolet. So do the yellow feathers in the crest of the sulphur-crested cockatoo. It is doubtful whether this property has any biological significance, but is simply a by-product of the chemical construction of the pigment synthesised chiefly by Australasian members of the family.

KEEPING THE PLUMAGE PUKKA

Like all birds, parrots need to keep their plumage in good serviceable order. Preening is by far the most common form of maintenance behaviour. The feathers are 'nibbled' through the beak, flakes of scale, parasites and dirt removed, and split vanes repaired by zipping the barbs and barbules together. Although macaws do not possess a preen gland, other parrots have very modest affairs. The secretion, when smeared over the plumage, helps to keep the feathers supple and waterproof. It also has bactericidal and fungicidal properties, so the oil may act as a disinfectant. Hygiene may be helped further by small fluffy feathers distributed all over the body, disintegrating and keeping the plumage well powdered.

A mated pair of
Masked lovebirds
preening each other.
(after Roger Stamm 1962)

Parrots also preen each other – allopreening. They give special attention to the head regions which tend to become dirty when the birds have been feeding on freely flowing nectar or pulpy fruit. Pesquet's parrot, an unusual lory-like parrot from the Papuan region, has virtually dispensed with feathers on its face thus giving it an unbecoming vulturine appearance; this may be in the interests of hygiene because the birds feed on messy fruit. However, all other parrots are faced with the problem of keeping their head plumage spick and span, and have evolved preening invitation postures whereby the head feathers are fully erected. This acts as an irresistible stimulus to a companion or sexual partner, and is usually successful in initiating a long bout of allopreening. This is why parrots like to have their heads tickled.

When given an opportunity, most parrots relish a bath. They prefer to stand in water and, by shuffling their wings, send droplets coursing through their plumage. Many kinds will even try and bathe on soaking wet foliage. Rain bathing has also been recorded for many members of the family. The behaviour can be quite spectacular as in the case of galahs. Although the onset of torrential rain will send many birds fleeing for cover, galahs in the bathing mood expose themselves to the downpour, stretching their wings, ruffling their plumage, and even hanging upside down, presumably allowing the water to trickle down against the lie of the feathers. On these occasions, the pink and grey cockatoos literally go swinging in the rain as though they really welcome a good soak after spending a hot dusty day in the Australian bush.

Scratching, too, is part of a parrot's toilet behaviour. It is very often a response to irritation on the bird's beak or head. The foot is also used to spread preen oil from the beak onto the rest of the body. Parrots have two methods of applying the foot to the plumage. The lories, cockatoos, macaws and the Afro-Asian parakeets scratch 'directly', ie the foot is brought straight up under the wing to meet the lowered head. Most other parrots raise the foot over the lowered wing, as most perching birds do. It was once thought that only those parrots which commonly hold food in the foot scratched 'under', but lories never 'handle' their food and yet use this method of scratching. The style may also change with age; nestling lovebirds scratch under their wing, but transfer to an overwing method after they fledge.

DESIGN FOR THE TREETOPS

The parrot's basic design for surviving in the upper storeys of forests is reflected not only in the colour of its feathers, but also in its anatomy. Like most birds, it relies greatly upon its legs to move around. A parrot's foot is specialised for the task of clenching and climbing. The majority of birds possess four toes on each foot, three pointing forwards and the first projecting to the rear so that it can work in opposition to the others. This arrangement enables birds to grip their perches. In some birds like owls and the fish-eating osprey, even the outer or fourth toe is capable of being rotated backwards to give the foot a yoke-toed configuration. In parrots, this arrangement is fixed, with the first and fourth toes permanently pointing backwards. It seems likely that this zygodactyl design is especially advantageous for

Upside down-like a bat! A Celebes Hanging Lorikeet at rest.

producing a firm, sure grip on twigs and branches. It is also as close as birds have come to evolving a manipulative 'hand', and enables parrots to cling upside down or sideways while grasping something with the other foot.

Yoke-toed feet appear in several other groups of arboreal birds, such as woodpeckers, barbets, toucans, touracos and trogons. Hornbills and kingfishers – a family that includes many woodland inhabitants – have their third and fourth toes partly joined to form a kind of sole. Both reptiles and mammals offer examples as well. Chameleons stalk their prey along branches held by their yoke-toed feet, and the koala has its five fingers divided into two opposable groups of three and two, which helps it to keep a tight grip high up in the tops of gum trees. We owe our own dexterity and fine manipulative abilities to our primate ancestors who evolved the grasping hand to steady themselves in the treetops and seize food. All these canopy dwellers independently developed similar solutions to the problem of how to maintain a confident footing among the foliage, a phenomenon called 'convergent evolution'.

Parrots walk or sidle rather than hop like finches, and their short legs (or tarsi) force them to waddle from side to side as the centre of gravity is alternately brought over each foot. This is also an integral part of their design for life in the trees; the squat legs keep the parrot's centre of gravity low down, and bestow upon the bird a short, and thus low geared, stride which makes climbing easy. But these birds have another trick to play when ascending the limbs of trees; they recruit their beak as a grappling hook. By anchoring its beak, and by the coordinated striding of its muscular neck and legs, a parrot can climb like a monkey. In this respect, parrots are unique.

The functioning of the bill as an extra 'foot' or 'hand' is made possible because the upper half has a very flexible attachment to the rest of the skull, enabling the mandibles to gape widely apart, so mimicking the prehensile action of the foot. Other kinds of birds possess only limited independent movement of their upper mandibles; they open their beaks by dropping the lower halves. However, in parrots, the mobility of the hooked upper jaw is particularly marked, enabling these birds to be amazingly adept at rotating and moving objects

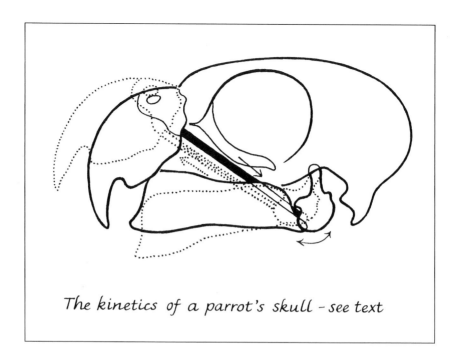

The kinetics of a parrot's skull - see text

around in their beaks. A glance at a parrot's skull reveals how this is achieved by a neat lever system. A loosely attached bone called the quadrate is located just below and forward of the ear canal. By the operation of special muscles, the quadrate can be swung backwards and forwards, and the movement transmitted to the upper jaw via a rod constructed from the zygomatic arch, the pterygoid and palatine bones. The upper beak is thus powered to open and close on a hinge-like joint in front of the brain case.

In spite of the fact that it bears a strong resemblance to the 'meat hook' of a bird of prey, the parrot's beak is quite different. Although its use as an ancillary foot is a bonus, its primary role, together with the muscular tongue, is that of an instrument for investigating, manipulating and preparing food.

A yellow-headed amazon showing its acrobatic ability, feeding in Costa Rica (K. White/ Bruce Coleman Ltd)

Varied lorikeet feeding on eucalypt pollen and nectar, Mount Isa, Australia (Hans and Judy Best/Ardea London Ltd)

THE BEAK, A GENTLE NUTCRACKER

No bird can rival the power of a large parrot's beak. If it had a mind to, a macaw or cockatoo could cut through fence wire with no difficulty. The palm cockatoo is equipped with a monstrous tool, well constructed to withstand the heavy loads generated during feeding, and yet its strength is achieved without incurring a heavy weight penalty. Although it appears to be very solid, the central core of the upper mandible is filled with a light lattice of fine bone struts which makes it immensely strong, as it needs to be, because these birds feed by crushing the nuts of pandanus palms. In the wild, other super-parrots use their beaks to assail the defences of heavily armoured seeds; it is no accident that Brazil nuts come from the Amazonian jungle where macaws live.

Parrots are fundamentally seed and fruit eaters, and their method of dealing with such food can be easily observed in a zoo. Given a handful of sunflower seeds, a medium-sized parrot can make short work of them. But it is the finesse of their feeding behaviour which is so fascinating. Although these birds can crack the hardest of nuts or reduce the wooden struts of their cages to a pile of splinters, they are able to separate the husks from the kernels with the utmost delicacy.

A seed, several of which can be stored in the bowl of the lower mandible, is firstly nudged forward by the tongue. Most birds possess flimsy, narrow tongues, but those of parrots bear an astonishing resemblance to muscular fingers, and are organs of great sensitivity as well. A parrot uses its tongue to probe for the weakest seam or best point of entry into a seed, and carefully fiddles it onto the broad overlapping surface of the upper mandible. This 'dental pad' is usually corrugated, and in the macaws has a distinct notch, helping to steady the seed. While the latter is kept in place by the tongue, which has a broad concave tip for the purpose, the lower mandible is brought into action, moving forward to bring the chisel-like edge to pare into the seed. With one movement, the husk can be split, such is the accuracy

Military macaw using its foot to 'handle' food, showing its powerful beak and muscular tongue (Rod Williams/Bruce Coleman Ltd)

with which a parrot can operate its formidable beak. Likewise the fleshy pericarps of fruit can be peeled away with a series of deft strokes of the lower mandible that would do justice to any chisel-wielding carpenter.

Like craftsmen, parrots need to look after their tools, devoting quite a lot of time to honing their beaks and keeping them clean and sharp. Parrots are accordingly ever nibbling even when there is nothing held between the tips of their mandibles. This behaviour helps to keep the continuously growing horny sheath worn down. Biting and chewing on hard objects such as pieces of wood also help to keep the cutting edges of the beak in good condition, and to exercise the powerful pinnate jaw muscles thus maintaining them in good trim. This habit is not always understood by the owners of pet parrots who accuse their charges of sheer vandalism when they rip into aviaries or household furniture. In fact, it is perfectly respectable parrot behaviour, designed to keep the beak in good condition.

Feeding also involves coordination between beak and feet. This is a skill which parrots share with only a very few birds and lends credence to their reputation as the monkeys of the bird world. A typical parrot involves its foot in one of two ways. It either uses it to clamp the food to the perch, or takes the food in it and offers it up to the beak in much the same way as we might eat a sandwich. The former method is referred to as 'tether-footed' and is widely employed by finches, tits, crows, birds of paradise and quail doves. Among the parrots, tether-footed feeding is more commonly displayed by the smaller kinds that thrive on grass seed, such as the budgerigar, Abyssinian lovebird and the small South American parakeets in the genus *Bolborhynchus*. This way of using the feet certainly helps these birds to hold down flexible grass stems while the seeds are extracted from the flowering heads or culms. In the second method, the morsel of food is generally plucked by the bill, and then transferred to the clenched 'fist'. Semi-aquatic gallinules feed like this as well as the large macaws, cockatoos, lories, lorikeets, amazons and rosellas. Keeping a grip on food using the feet may well have survival value in the swaying tops of trees.

PUTTING POLLY'S BEST FOOT FORWARD

Like humans, parrots put the best 'hand' or foot forward. A study of a captive black-headed caique revealed that the bird was strongly right footed, taking and holding food in the right foot on 76 out of 100 times. When offered tasty morsels from the left, it still managed to take the rewards with the right foot on 62 per cent of the tests; not surprisingly, when food was presented to it from the right-hand side, the parrot snatched it almost exclusively with the right foot – at least on 96 per cent of the tests. Footedness varies from bird to bird; out of a flock of 56 brown-throated conures exactly half preferred to use their right foot, and the other half were left footed. Another study of cockatoos indicated that three-quarters of them were left footed. (By comparison, all but 5 per cent of the human race are right handed.) There is even evidence that wild parrots favour one side or the other. An eclectus parrot 'collected' in the field was found to have a crop crammed with red fruit, and the incriminating stain on the right foot revealed that it was decidedly right footed.

This behaviour seems to be firmly entrenched in the neural circuits because attempts to train parrots into changing their footedness have met with only limited success. For example, a young right-footed blue-rumped parrot was persistently fed from the left. It eventually learned to take some of the food with its left foot, but after a few seconds it would transfer the offering to its dominant right one. Even parrots, it seems, cannot be forced into becoming 'cack-handed'.

PARROTS OF ALL SIZES

One measure of success that can be applied to a group of animals is to see to what extent they have been opportunistic in evolutionary terms. On this score, parrots rate well with 333 different kinds ranging from the metre-long hyacinth and scarlet macaws to the wren-sized pygmy parrots of the Papuan region. The ten-fold size range between these tiny creatures and the super-parrots alone suggests that these birds have been able to exploit a whole range of life-styles. Speciation has also been helped by the fact that parrots range broadly over the separate continents in the southern hemisphere, with populations kept apart by sea and mountain barriers. This kind of separation is a potent factor in the creation of species. Parrots have certainly benefited in this respect, but there are other considerations which may have enabled them to reach the full potential of their design.

The absence of terrestrial mammals in New Zealand literally left the field wide open for birds like moas to take over the role of herbivores. With no rapacious carnivores to contend with, they and other kinds of birds had no need for flight, and so were free to capitalize upon the advantages of size as a means of increasing their biological efficiency. A parrot, the kakapo, filled the niche that in other parts of the world was taken by the rabbit. It is one of the most remarkable members of the family with a lekking arrangement for courting (see Chapter 3) and can, like so many of New Zealand's indigenous birds, fly only downhill!

Apart from bats, seals and the odd rodent, the Australian mainland never hosted a placental mammal until man and his hangers-on stepped ashore more than 45,000 years ago. Parrots therefore enjoyed a halcyon existence without ruthlessly efficient cats, dogs and small mustelids (weasel-like carnivores); even the absence of tree-dwelling primates and rodents with their taste for seeds and fruits must have made life considerably less competitive for parrots, and facilitated a biological explosion in that part of the world, producing cockatoos, broad-tailed parrots (eg rosellas), grass parakeets (eg budgerigars), fig-eaters or lorilets, lories and lorikeets, the ground-dwelling and nocturnal night parrot and the amazon-like eclectus. The wonderful diversity of parrot types is largely a reflection of their different dietary requirements.

PARROTS AND PLANTS

Parrots are basically seed predators, the dimension of their beaks determining the size of the seeds that they can crack. The smaller ones, like budgies, lovebirds and parrotlets from South America, seek grains of grass and herbs, while the mighty macaws make short work of reinforced nuts that barely yield to a sledge-hammer.

There is little doubt as to the power of parrots to divest plants of their seeds. The seed crop of some rainforest trees, like the Costa Rican pea tree, *Hymenolobium*, is measured in tens of thousands a year, and yet it takes parrots and toucans just two weeks to strip such a tree of its crop. While the tree is in fruit, flocks of excited red-lored parrots swoop into the ten-storey-high canopy, flashing their green and red plumage and jockeying for position on the branches laden with long pods. Then the feast begins; each bird grabs a stalk, severing it with the strong bill while holding the pod with one foot. It then slits the pod, after which it extracts the seeds deftly with tongue and beak. With such efficient eaters, it is a wonder that any seeds manage to escape. As it is, it is possible that some jungle plants have to produce 50 million seeds in order that one will survive to maturity.

But plants do not willingly make such nourishing wares just to improve the quality of life for birds like parrots, far from it. As a family, parrots have muscled in on a mutually beneficial partnership that has been forged between some plants and certain kinds of birds. The relationship evolved because plants have one great weakness, they cannot move. This means that they must find a way of dispersing their seeds so that the offspring do not wither in the shadow of their parents. Some plants use wind and water to transport their seeds to fresh pastures; but many others have developed ways of enticing animals to be the unwitting agents for their dispersal. Some provide edible structures, like the red arils of yew or the eye-catching arils of acacias which tempt birds to swallow and transport the seeds in their guts. Many others package their seeds in colourful and succulent flesh, forming berries and drupes. Fruits like figs are designed to be devoured, but the seeds are built to withstand the grinding action of the gizzard and the corrosive effect of the digestive juices so that they are voided or simply dropped unscathed well away from the parent plant. In the development of such packaging the plant is, however, faced with a dilemma – it needs birds and mammals to consume its fruit, but not at the expense of destroying the seeds, which must themselves be packed with nourishing endosperm to give the young plant a good start in life.

Parrots have different objectives. While having a taste for fruit pulp, many are able to fracture the seed coats with their beaks, or grind them to a mush inside their immensely muscular gizzards. Parrots are therefore able to plunder the resources that plants lay up for their growing seedlings. In Australia, this is the fate of the mistletoes. Two kinds of birds live on the glutinous berries, the appropriately named mistletoe bird and the painted honeyeater, digesting the sticky outer flesh but excreting the stone-like seeds unharmed. However, when parrots tackle the ripe berries, they take everything, precious seed included. Pressure like this exerted upon plants by gluttonous seed eaters has consequently resulted in an 'arms race'. To discourage this kind of cheating, plants either place their seeds in greatly reinforced shells or pack them with unpalatable or poisonous chemicals. These two strategies produced the armoured Brazil nut on the one hand and, on the other, the highly distasteful chilli pepper, the seeds of which are blisteringly hot.

Scarlet macaws, currently under investigation in Peru's remote and magnificent Manu National Park, eat between forty and fifty kinds of fruit and nuts, many of which are so noxious that most other animals would not even try to tackle them. The seeds of some species are enclosed in pods of iron-like consistency which the scientists themselves took nearly an hour to crack open; and yet the macaws take all of four seconds to remove the edible seeds from their pod-fortress. These and other parrots also consume seeds protected inside fruit that appear to be unattractive to other animals. For example, the poisonous seeds of the soap-box tree are encased in iron-hard fruits that 'explode' when they are ripe, jettisoning the contents at 96km (60 miles) an hour. Also, those of the Parkia tree are protected inside pods of leather-like consistency. Macaws love both kinds of seeds which they obtain easily by chewing into the protective packaging.

The lowland mahogany produces large numbers of small winged seeds. They are so bitter that macaws are apparently one of the very few vertebrates that can cope with them. To put off potential seed predators, the mahogany lays down defensive chemicals – alkaloids, tannins and the like – which play havoc with the digestion. Most animals wisely give these seeds a wide berth. Parrots are also able to beat the competitors to sources of food by consuming fruit and seeds before they are ripe. These are generally protected by bitter tannins which disappear as the fruit ripens; but as parrots and macaws are able to eat toxic seeds, the tannins are no real deterrent to these birds. From their diet, it is apparent that large macaws possess iron-clad digestion. Indeed, the ability to ingest toxin-laden seeds and fruit may account for their taste for clay.

Distributed around Manu National Park are many exposed banks of salt-rich soil that are visited daily by large numbers of parrots, including scarlet and red and green macaws, blue-headed, orange-cheeked and mealy parrots. By carefully monitoring the macaws (they can be individually recognised by their face markings) – scientists have discovered that each bird visits one of these salt licks about three times a week. Early in the morning when it is hot and sticky, parties of parrots begin to gather in the trees around the patches of bare ground. The macaws are especially nervous, and may spend three or more hours loafing before eventually flying down. Each macaw then sets to work scooping up chunks of earth and swallowing what it can before the lumps crumble and spill onto the ground. The Andean Indians provide a clue to the function of this behaviour, because they eat clay to protect themselves against hazardous alkaloids in wild potatoes. Furthermore, it is known that kaolin, a very fine clay, contains various minerals which chemically bind to and neutralise toxic substances. In other parts of the world, seed and leaf eating animals require extra salts to help their assimilation of mildly toxic food, so perhaps the regular visits by macaws and other parrots to these salt licks may help them to overcome the poisons in their food.

The relationship between parrots and plants is echoed in Australasia, but with further refinements. Over the course of 50 million years of isolation the ancestors of the parrots, pigeons, lyre birds, bower birds and honeyeaters interacted with the original eucalypts (gum trees), proteas and mistletoes, and affected the course of each other's evolution. In Australia, over 1,000 kinds of plants entice birds to pollinate their flowers by offering them bribes of nectar, recruiting birds for this purpose because they have certain advantages over insects as couriers of pollen. While insects tend to be sluggish during cool weather, birds are active every day. Also, Australia was rather poorly endowed with native social bees. In their insatiable quest for food, parrots capitalized upon this situation and the specialised and highly successful lories and lorikeets are the result.

Nectar is an energy-rich source of nourishment, consisting mostly of the sugars, fructose and glucose, in solution. Furthermore, it is easily absorbed into the bloodstream. However, a year-round diet consisting solely of nectar would be very unbalanced and so the flower-feeding parrots take insects, fruit and substantial amounts of protein-rich pollen, to the plant's detriment. Indeed, some people believe that pollen may be more important than the sugary fluid, at least to lories and lorikeets.

Several families of birds do thrive chiefly upon nectar. Best known are the 319 kinds of hummingbirds which obtain most of their sustenance by hovering, with whirring wings like giant moths, in front of blooms. 'Docking' with the nectaries, they use their long tongues to withdraw the equivalent of half their body weight of nectar each day. In the Old World their place is taken by the glossy but unrelated sunbirds. The honeyeaters are the dominant nectar feeders in Australia, New Zealand and the south-west Pacific where they vie with the dazzling lories, lorikeets and the migratory swift parrot for what flowers have to offer.

In Australia, the eucalypts provide a particularly rich source for these parrots. The 450-600 species belong to the myrtle family, and dominate the landscape with their characteristic loose-limbed shapes and blue-green foliage. They vary in size from the bush-like mallee, adapted to life in the arid centre of the continent, to the lordly mountain ashes soaring 90m (300ft) into the sky. Although some flower irregularly, when they do their brilliant white, cream and crimson blossoms set the trees alight with colour. Each flower is constructed like an open brush of exposed anthers into which the avian customers need to delve in order to discover the nectaries, getting their faces thoroughly dusted with pollen in the process. As birds have a far greater thirst than insects, each eucalypt flower secretes large quantities of nectar to make the bird's visit worthwhile. However, the yield per flower does vary from one kind of gum to another. For example, the messmate, *E. obliqua* – the first kind of gum tree recorded by the European visitors – produces in energy terms 6-10 joules a day, whereas

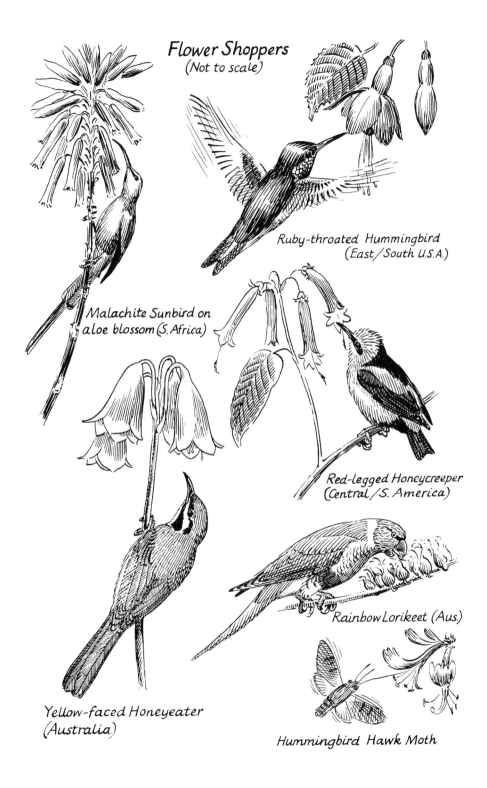

Flower Shoppers
(Not to scale)

Ruby-throated Hummingbird
(East/South U.S.A.)

Malachite Sunbird on
aloe blossom (S. Africa)

Red-legged Honeycreeper
(Central/S. America)

Rainbow Lorikeet (Aus.)

Yellow-faced Honeyeater
(Australia)

Hummingbird Hawk Moth

in *E. cosmophylla*, the daily output is a staggering 200-400 joules per flower. The flowers are also long lived, some surviving for nearly a month. Such examples may well produce up to 6,000 joules of nectar, and attract 1,000 visits by pollen and nectar seeking creatures.

When the flow is good, the trees literally drip nectar, and the canopies become alive with activity as insects and birds home in on the honeypots; everywhere, multi-coloured, chirruping lorikeets like rainbows cascade out of the sky as they move from one grove to another, their necks often smeared with treacle-like fluid and plastered with pollen. Should the nectar become slightly fermented, the birds can become somewhat inebriated on the mead-like drink and unable to fly. Unlike the honeyeaters, the lorikeets and other opportunistic parrots which fly in for the feast tend to destroy many of the flowers by chewing into the clusters of anthers in order to collect the pollen and to derive nourishment from the developing ovules.

Rainbow lorikeet using its brush tongue to collect pollen and nectar. The papillae on the tip of the tongue are erectile.

'Flower shopping' has had important consequences for the lories and lorikeets of Australasia. Each is equipped with a bill which is not particularly powerful, having no file-like grooves on the under surface of the upper mandible. However, their tongue is quite unlike that of other parrots, being furnished with a tuft of papillae, thus accounting for the lorikeet's scientific name, *Trichoglossus*, meaning 'hair-tongued'. These papillae are enclosed by a sheath when the bird is at rest or feeding on fruit or seeds, but become expanded like the tentacles of a sea anemone when the tongue is being employed for feeding on flowers. They are arranged into a fringe around the tip, making the tongue an efficient fluid collector, operating like a paint brush which draws up liquid by capillary attraction. It has also been suggested that the brush tongue is designed to harvest the powdery pollen and compress it into a form more suitable for swallowing. In captivity both lories and lorikeets use their tongues for scooping the pulp out of soft fruit and, incidentally, will strip green bark from twigs. As might be expected, their gizzards are feeble because they have no need for an internal mill for crushing reinforced seeds, but they all possess capacious crops which are used for storing and absorbing nectar.

There is a disadvantage in relying upon blossoms for nourishment. Few of the plants on which these parrots depend have regular flowering seasons; the production of nectar and pollen therefore varies from year to year. Consequently, lories and lorikeets tend to be very nomadic and breed opportunistically wherever and whenever the trees are sufficiently in bloom to support the extra demands of rearing families. In practice, peak nesting tends to occur in the wet season which corresponds to the time when the trees and shrubs come into flower. However, the absence of a well-defined nesting season favours permanent pairing so that the birds are ready to breed with the minimum of delay.

Parrots must also have exerted considerable pressure on Australian plants inducing them to safeguard their seeds with hard coats or to place them inside tough, woody cones. Cockatoos and gum nuts may well be the outcome of this antipodean 'arms race'. The tiny capsules from which the sprays of anthers emerge are destined to become the fruits of the eucalyptus trees. These hold the seeds and as they

Red-capped Parrot extracting seeds from seed-capsule of the Marri
(Eucalyptus calophylla). Detail shows elongated upper mandible.

develop, the urns change from being soft and pliable to a wood-like consistency. When mature, the top of the capsule opens, and the seeds are liberated. Although the armoured fruits offer protection to the seeds from the smaller parrots, many fall to the hefty bills of cockatoos which crush the capsules in an instance. Some eucalypts such as the marri, *E. calophylla*, a gum from the Stirling Range in Western Australia, produces large urns of great strength, yet there are parrots that have managed to crack even them. The solution to the problem of extracting the seeds is to winkle them out through the lip of the capsule which is normally sealed by a lid; several kinds of parrot are able to do this through the evolution of specially shaped beaks. The red-capped parrot has an upper mandible shaped like a long curved spike which it inserts into the marri nut to withdraw the seeds. Two kinds of black cockatoo are also able to exploit these seeds in south-west Australia – the long-billed black and the long-billed form of the red-tailed black. These super-parrots are able, by sheer force, to chew through the base of the capsules and extract the contents.

All the black cockatoos are characterised by their different bill shapes and these enable them to specialise. The relatively slender one of the funereal cockatoo is deployed to extract seeds from the cones of Banksias, pines etc. Most populations of red-tailed blacks possess short, broad bills that are better suited to crushing woody fruit, while the massive beak of the glossy black cockatoo, which gives the bird a comical appearance, is used to tear apart the cones of casuarina trees.

WOODPECKER PARROTS

Like all cockatoos, blacks have an appetite for grubs and, given a chance, will strip away bark and tear out rotten wood in their search for the boring larvae of beetles and moths.. In this respect, they are taking on the role of woodpeckers which are absent from Australia. The fat and juicy larvae of the cossid moth, *Xyleutes boisduvali*, are particularly liked by the yellow-tailed black cockatoo; these wood-boring insects do a great deal of damage to gum trees grown for wood pulp. When hunting, the big black cockatoos enter the plantations and cling to the trunks listening for the noise of the grubs as they chew

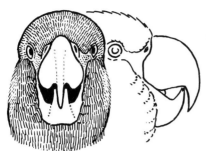

Yellow-tailed Black Cockatoo
(C. f. funereus)

Long-billed Black Cockatoo
(C. f. baudinii)

Red-tailed Black Cockatoo
(C. m. magnificus)

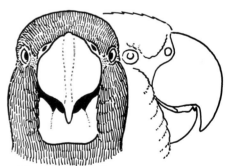

Glossy Black Cockatoo
(C. lathami)

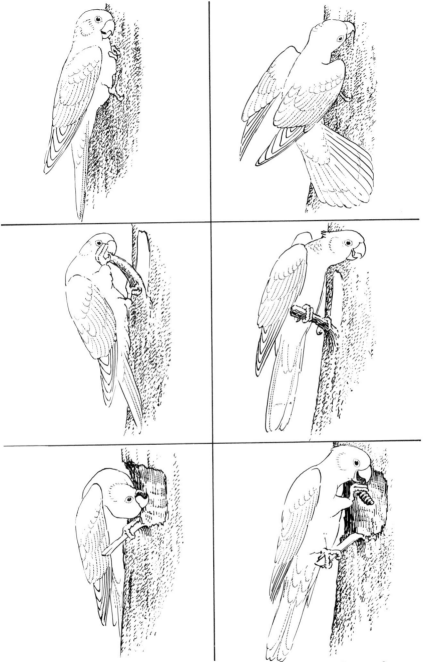

Yellow-tailed Black Cockatoo extracting a Cossid Moth larva from its gallery in a tree trunk.
(Based on illustrations in Aust. Wildl. Res. 1978. 5. McInnes & Carne)

A pair of
Buff-faced
Pygmy Parrots

out the wood in their galleries. On locating an active grub, the parrot peels away the bark, making a perch for itself, and then gouges out wedges of wood to expose the prey. Up to 40 per cent of trees may sustain serious damage from the activities of both larvae and cockatoos.

The smallest parrots in the world behave in a way reminiscent of woodpeckers or tree creepers, indeed the six species which are confined to the forests of the Papuan region are sometimes referred to as woodpecker parrots. Like woodpeckers they have stiffened tail feathers with the shafts extending beyond the ends of the vanes to act as props, supporting the weight of these tiny birds while they scamper around the tree trunks. They also possess very long toes and claws to help them gain a good purchase on bark. Although they have relatively powerful beaks for their size, similar in structure to those of cockatoos, pygmy parrots do not appear to use them for macerating wood. Indeed, for many years their diet was a mystery because all attempts to keep them alive in captivity on fruit and insects met with dismal success. Post-mortem examination of their stomach contents usually revealed a sticky white mass. However, recent observations of

54

these puny parrots in New Guinea indicate that they may be fungus foragers, taking lichens, small insects and perhaps seeds suited to their size.

PARROTS FOR PLOUGHING

Some parrots have taken to feeding chiefly on the ground and this has led to interesting changes in their design. Many of the cockatoos are at home both in trees or on the ground. The 'white' cockatoos, for instance, can dig with their beaks, and will pull cow-pats apart to look for larvae. The galah is also fairly terrestrial but tends to take seeds, sprouting crops and insect larvae that are already exposed. On the other hand, the corellas are much more adept at digging and therefore are able to cash in on a ready supply of roots, bulbs and grubs normally concealed beneath the surface of the soil. The slender-billed corella has a long, forward-projecting upper mandible which functions as a

Long-billed Corellas using their beaks for digging out corms

55

trowel. When fossicking, the birds move backwards and use the upper beak to plough a furrow, thus exposing anything which may be edible. These birds are particularly keen on the little bulbs of the introduced onion grass, which they dig up with their beaks.

The kea from New Zealand is another trowel-beaked species, the beak being much longer in the cock birds. Like the corellas, the kea spends much of its time foraging on the ground, grubbing up roots and fossorial invertebrates. However, being omnivorous and no less opportunistic than most parrots, it took advantage of the abundant carrion generated by New Zealand's 50 million sheep. Its role as a scavenger of carcases was greatly assisted by the heavily decurved beak that doubles up as a meat-hook comparable with that of an eagle's. In fact, it is very tempting to regard the kea as the parrot's answer to a buzzard or at least a raven.

GROUNDED PARROTS

Two kinds of parrots in Australia tend to keep their feet firmly in contact with terra firma. The ground parrot, nearly twice the size of a budgerigar, is moss green, and is confined to heathlands and swamps chiefly on the east coast. It has the habits of a quail. Being shy, elusive, and nocturnal to boot, it comes to light only when flushed. Even so, it prefers to run on legs that are as long as those of plovers rather than fly. Its close relative, the night parrot, has been called Australia's most mysterious bird. Confined to the spinnifex areas of the arid centre, this species is rarely seen; indeed, only one specimen has ever been taken and that was in 1912. However, the 23cm (9in) long birds are masters of camouflage, each feather being green with the centres spotted dark brown and yellow. In the vast areas covered with spinnifex grass, it would be easier looking for a needle in a haystack.

By far the most interesting of the ground-dwelling parrots is the kakapo from New Zealand, a cat-sized species which has all but lost the power of flight. With its breast muscles accounting for only 3 per cent of its total weight, the best this bird can achieve is a 'controlled free fall'. Tipping the scales at 3kg (6.6lb), a cock kakapo rates as the heaviest of parrots. When other respectable parrots are going about their business, the few remaining kakapo are roosting in hollows beneath trees or boulders. As night falls, they waken and waddle along established paths trampled through the lush vegetation to their feeding stations. Here they nibble ferns, grasses and bulbs, and even climb trees such as ratas for their nectar. Wherever they feed they leave little balls of fibre, having chewed the goodness out of the vegetation.

Although the kakapo can be regarded in ecological terms as a 'parrot rabbit', in looks it is reminiscent of an owl, with an arrangement of small feathers around the eyes forming quite distinct facial discs. Furthermore, filamentous extensions of the feathers at the base of the bill are similar in appearance to whiskers. Perhaps these are touch receptors to help the birds locate obstacles in the dark. Like the ground parrot, the kakapo is a 'perfumed parrot' and seems able to scent-mark its surroundings; dogs can quickly find them. The use of aromatic chemicals in this way is a very mammalian characteristic.

So much for parrot diversity; now for parrots at home.

Palm Cockatoo using stick to beat
dead branch like a drum

3·PARROT SEX AND SOCIETY

In March 1981, a mysterious loud tapping was heard in the Iron Range, in the north-eastern part of Cape York Peninsula, Australia. On investigation, the instrumentalist proved to be a male palm cockatoo. He had adopted a heraldic posture while pirouetting on top of a dead eucalypt trunk. His cheeks were flushed with blood, and the glossy black wings were outstretched; the drumming came from a hollow branch which the bizarre cockatoo was hitting with a stick clenched in his left foot. The astonishing display lasted for a minute or more, and was followed by the bird rolling his head forward, a gesture made all the more spectacular by the erection of the shaggy crest. Meanwhile, the other member of the pair had been eyeing the activity from a nearby vantage point, and was sufficiently impressed by it to fly down and caress the drummer on his neck.

Apart from being a remarkable example of tool using by a bird – the 'drumsticks' are specially prepared and stored – nobody had witnessed this behaviour before. Since then, palm cockatoos have been regularly observed drumming tattoos on resonant branches, and their performances have even been filmed. But why should these birds have mastered the art of percussion? The most likely explanation is that the ritual has a social or sexual message, perhaps a territorial acclamation of the kind that woodpeckers generate, although in their case, the drumming is made by striking their beaks onto the sides of trees.

Parrots are nothing if not social birds, with a need for each other's company and for keeping in touch by vocal and visual means. This enables them to survive and breed.

59

SAFETY IN NUMBERS

Parrots of a feather, tend to flock together. Sometimes, as in the case of many forest species, these birds go about their daily business in family groups, commuting from their roosting quarters to their feeding areas, and back again by nightfall. Parrots that live in more open and arid areas gather in spectacular mobs. For example, when the country-side is becoming parched in the centre of Australia, budgerigars occasionally assemble in green blizzards around the last remaining watering holes. They appear first as a dark smudge on the horizon that changes shape, undulating this way and that. Then the chirruping birds sweep low through the trees and in an instant, as if of one mind, settle on the gaunt forms of trees surrounding the water. Silence reigns. Suddenly, all is action. The birds pour from the air in a green mass of budgerigars as though from a flask. As the edges of the pool fill up, succeeding birds rain down directly onto the surface where they lie spread-eagled while they take their fill of muddy water, thereby ensuring their survival for another day or two. When the birds become too desperate for a drink, many drown in reservoirs and water tanks. When the Trans-Australian Railway was being built, 5 tons of budgies and other parrots were taken from a dam at Kingoonya Station. Cockatoos also occur in vast mobs; attracted by the easy pickings of cereals, 4,000–8,000 red-tailed blacks occasionally descend on Kununurra, and enormous flocks of up to 70,000 little corellas occur in the north west. They have good reasons for being sociable, because even the largest parrots can be plucked from the air by birds of prey.

Although parrots may look as though they can defend themselves with their massive hooked beaks, they have the look of the hunted with eyes set on either side of the head to give them good all round vision and fair warning of danger. However, the more pairs of eyes scanning the skies, the better. Here lies the advantage of birds moving about in flocks. With so many vigilant individuals on the lookout, it is very difficult for predators to take them by surprise. Hawks and falcons probably find large swirling flocks of prey confusing, causing them to be less successful in singling out victims. Certainly, little and black falcons have to work quite hard to pluck budgerigars out of the flocks

Safety in numbers. A Brown Falcon is confused by a wheeling flock of Budgerigars.

milling around drinking places. From the individual parrot's point of view, the 'safety in numbers' principle is firmly based upon selfishness; by 'hiding' among its numerous flock-mates, it hopes to maximise its chances of survival.

Flocking requires discipline. A party of parrots must, by definition, act in concert, and this is achieved by a phenomenon called 'social facilitation'. A clannish parrot is fundamentally a 'copy cat', and will tend to adopt the activity its companions are engaged in, feeding when they feed, bathing when they are giving themselves a soaking, and flying when they take off. This urge to conform is crucial for birds in which togetherness is the key to survival. Communication plays a role in maintaining the cohesion of the flocks. Parrots, like most sociable species, are furnished with a set of body signals which help to coordinate the behaviour of the birds within the flock. Best known are 'flash markings', which are the outcome of an evolutionary dilemma. On the one hand, parrots are under pressure to remain concealed from predators, which accounts for their generally camouflaged colouring;

on the other hand, being gregarious creatures, they need to pass messages to each other by means of readily observable signals. The solution is to keep the colourful signs hidden, only showing them off when circumstances merit.

Most parrots possess a combination of vividly coloured tails, rumps, fore- and underwings. Although normally covered, they are revealed to startling effect when the birds become airborne. These patches of colour usually contrast with the rest of the plumage to add impact to the signals. For example, black cockatoos reveal flashes of red or yellow on the sides of their tails when in flight. The budgerigar's wings and tail feathers are black and yellow and are quite startling when spread. A patch of fabulous electric blue is exposed on the rump when a crimson-winged parrot launches itself into the air, and the effect is further enhanced by its brilliant red wings. Meyer's parrots from the southern part of Africa display kingfisher blue rumps when they fly. Many amazons have areas of red, yellow and blue on their flight feathers, resembling national insignia on the wings of military aircraft. The orange-winged amazon, for example, reveals splashes of reddish orange set off with yellow on the outer secondary pinions rather similar to roundels. The very sociable rainbow lorikeet exposes an eye-catching pattern of yellow and black on the primary wing feathers and reveals scarlet underwing coverts as well. Even the drab kea keeps a surprise beneath its wings, with flashes of tangerine orange.

Parrots on the move are therefore meant to be seen, and explode into blazes of colour or dazzling patterns when they take to their wings, making it easy for flock-mates to follow and keep together. These visual signals are further supplemented by shrill contact calls which differ from species to species, and effectively say 'Here I am, where are you?'

PROVOCATIVE PARROTS

Like all social creatures, parrots have evolved a range of behaviour to establish and strengthen social bonds and to smooth interactions between the members of a flock. But like all creatures they must secure valuable resources like food, perches and mates and, if necessary, fight for them. Assertive and appeasement conventions are therefore of great importance in enabling disputes to be settled quickly by an exchange of signals rather than through murderous fights.

Like most birds, a parrot intimidates a competitor by threatening to use its chief weapon – its beak. This is potentially a dangerous instrument which, if its 'fire power' is fully unleashed, can inflict a great deal of damage on the sparring partner. However, quarrelling parrots tend to pull their punches by adopting ritualised postures. Threat usually involves pointing the beak at an opponent and gaping which is itself an 'inhibited' bite – the greater the anger, the wider the gape. The gregarious parrots tend to keep their aggression more in check than the less social kinds. For example, the intensely social white-eye-ringed kinds of lovebirds and the peach-faced, are very reluctant to bite each other, whereas the more solitary Madagascan lovebird often launches straight into an attack on the toes of its adversaries. If the opponent stands its ground, the behaviour escalates into a sparring contest with the birds partially locking their beaks. However, even these vicious looking duels rarely result in injury; the fighting has become largely stylized into wrestles of strength and endurance, rather than disputes to the death.

There is also evidence that parrots with big bills tend to avoid fights. James Serpell, a zoologist from Cambridge, studied the aggressive behaviour of several kinds of lorikeets. Some had relatively small and weak beaks while others had large ones capable of splintering wood. He used a mirror to wind up his birds – a standard ploy for deceiving birds into thinking that they are confronted with an angry-looking aggressor. Although the lorikeets with the weakest bills readily sparred with their reflection, those equipped with the most formidable weapons were reluctant to attack, but postured in a very complex way.

It is a well known fact of animal behaviour that threat behaviour becomes more complex as fighting becomes more dangerous. Oxford zoologists, Richard Dawkins and John Krebs, suggested in 1978 that involved displays allow an animal to escalate threats gradually before resorting to costly violence. So parrots with powerful beaks need a greater range of threat signals to communicate stages of anger. The

Two of 30 different postures
that Rainbow Lorikeets
use to intimidate rivals
(after James Serpell)

large-billed lorikeets achieve this by using a great variety of discreet gestures but in a haphazard order. Switching between these in an unpredictable manner may be more frightening than repeating a few clichéd displays over and over again. Serpell thinks the superior lorikeet may be especially expert at 'dazzling rivals with the unexpectedness, speed, and intricacy of its displays'.

In many kinds of parrots, the impact of threat behaviour has been enhanced by the evolution of colour patterns which make the frontal presentation of the bill more intimidating. In all lovebirds, except the Madagascan, the beak is red and contrasts markedly with the face coloration. In the orange-chinned parakeet from Central America, the feathers on either side of the chin – the malar ruff – are raised to impart a bearded appearance to a threatening bird. In fact any decoration around the beak or on the face will tend to emphasise the warning gesture, forming a 'fright mask' to scare opponents into submission.

Parrots also wield their wingbutts or carpals to threaten each other. The gesture is almost certainly derived from a flight intention movement, and warns rivals that the aggressor is likely to fly into an attack. When annoyed, yellow-winged and orange-chinned parakeets jerk their 'wrists' away from their flanks. It may be no accident that many parrots have brightly adorned edges to the forewings, and these would be revealed by carpal-flashing. For example, the wingbutts of Meyer's parrot are bright yellow, which contrasts markedly with the grey upper plumage. In the Abyssinian lovebird, the area exposed by this action is black so that when seen from the front the signal appears as a pair of dark flashes against green plumage. The correlation between wing coloration and the use of the wings for threatening is well illustrated by the little hanging lorikeets. They use a rapid raising and lowering of the folded wings to encourage others to keep their distance. In the vernal and blue-crowned hanging lorikeets, the wing flicks are made conspicuous by the presence of iridescent blue and black coloration on the under surfaces. They also flash their carpals, and both the Moluccan and Celebes species possess red 'wrists' which give force to the intimidating display.

APPEASING PARROTS

Parrots also possess ways of appeasing angry companions; this ability is obviously important for gregarious animals. Flight and withdrawal in the face of an attack are simple and effective ways of conceding defeat. A parrot can also calm down an aggressor by the nature of its plumage posture. A submissive and non-assertive individual withdraws its neck and fluffs out its feathers, signalling that it poses no threat to anyone. Sick and inactive birds often assume a rounded, dozy form, showing that they are incapable of making trouble. When tempers are aroused, hiding the bill is another effective act of appeasement. Since brandishing the beak is a provocative act between parrots, removing it and the 'fright mask' from view has a soothing effect. By head flagging or 'turning the cheek' a parrot communicates its desire to flee and avoid conflict. Again, the impact of this behaviour may be increased by exhibiting a patch of colour on the nape, as in several of the Australian broad-tailed parrots. But most members of the parrot family have another method of appeasement from which the cockatoo's cheeky crests may have arisen – inviting social preening.

On the whole, birds do not tolerate bodily contact in non-mating situations, but surround themselves with a 'personal space' from which they repel all trespassers; swallows spaced out on a telegraph wire illustrate birds defending areas in the immediate vicinity of themselves. However, most parrots are 'contact' species and, when resting, tend to seek out their companions or mates and sit with their flanks pressing against each other. However, intrusion into a neighbour's personal space to 'snuggle' up to it is likely to arouse strong feelings of hostility or even fear. In this context, the grooming invitation posture with head feathers raised is designed to suppress such anti-social influences and replace them with friendly grooming. The proffered head with plumage fully erected is an important gesture towards keeping the peace in many parrot societies. Furthermore, the long bouts of mutual preening that the behaviour initiates may strengthen the bond between mates.

Generalised head ruffling is found in many parrots, but not in the Australian broad-tailed which keep their distance from each other. However, in crested cockatoos, head plumage erection is taken to dramatic extremes. Structural changes in the feathers, the development of vivid colours and the ability to generate an exaggerated pilomotor response have all contributed to the evolution of crests. They vary from the mundane to the magnificent. Galahs simply possess elongated crown feathers which, when erected in excitement or when landing as a greeting, make the head look taller. The palm cockatoo has a cascade of spiky black plumes that can be raised or lowered at will. More sophisticated ones are found in the sulphur-crested and pink cockatoos. The former has brilliant yellow plumes overlaid with white feathers when the crest is closed. In Major Mitchell's cockatoo, the erected crest is breath-taking when flourished with a series of head nods – the fan reveals concentric red and yellow bands. Such crests are designed to be shown off in profile. However, the South American

Palm Cockatoo

Major Mitchell's
Cockatoo

Gang-gang Cockatoo

Cockatiel

White Cockatoo

Hawk-headed Parrot

hawk-headed parrot sports a crest which is meant to be seen head on. Many of the amazons to which it is related seem to possess cape-like plumage on the neck which is often distinctively patterned; from such an arrangement the hawk-headed parrot has evolved a wonderful ruff of rich maroon feathers edged in blue. When spread out, the effect is startling, the whole head becoming framed by a great fan of feathers. Frontal displays have also evolved from the basic cockatoo's crest. The Moluccan or red-vented cockatoo has a backward curving, floppy crest of yellow and rose pink; when raised, the broad feathers are supplemented by the laterally spread cheek and malar plumage.

The necklace of spots which gives a cock Budgerigar sex-appeal

Observed from the front, the forehead is greatly heightened by the crest, and the face swells to dramatic proportions. Even in the non-crested budgerigar, the yellow forehead plumage can be erected, and the feathers of the cheeks and chin fanned sideways. The black spots and the purple moustache stripes add impact to the display.

Cockatoos appear to raise their crests in various contexts – when alarmed, on landing and during moments of sexual excitement. In all these situations, the birds are strongly aroused. Cockatoos also proffer their crests for grooming. What started out as a generalised grooming invitation posture, became moulded and fashioned by natural selection into a dramatic social and sexual signal. The groups in which parrots usually live are not only socially stimulating, they also provide plenty of choice when it comes to selecting a mate. As the breeding season approaches, the presence of so many sexually aroused companions provides the eroticism and stimulation for successful pairing. As aviculturists confirm, in many species a lone pair of parrots are often bored and barren.

SEX AND THE SOCIAL PARROT

In their sexual relationships, many parrots seem to be paragons of virtue. They have a reputation for being faithfully monogamous although in one population of corellas monitored by Graeme Smith in

68

Western Australia, 40 per cent of the pairs divorced on a regular basis, and produced a tangle of relationships worthy of a television soap opera. The break-ups were unconnected with breeding failure. Parrots are not great home builders, nesting in holes already constructed for them. Only the hen incubates the white eggs, during which time she is fed by her mate. The whole breeding cycle is often comparatively long, taking five months in the case of the yellow-tailed black cockatoo. After fledging, the young may be dependent upon the parents for many months. There are, however, many interesting exceptions to this thumbnail sketch of the parrot's family life.

Although cock parrots tend to be more vividly attired, slightly heavier, and possess proportionately heftier beaks than their mates, the sexes in most species show only feeble distinctions. This unisex coloration may be related to the fact that many parrots establish fairly permanent pair bonds as soon as they are mature. Thereafter, a parrot's mate is its most important 'friend', until death parts them. By day, they accompany each other to feeding sites, even within a large flock, and satisfy their hunger in each other's presence. When satiated, the mates then loaf around, grooming and responding to each other's preening invitation displays; doubtless this affectionate behaviour strengthens the relationship between the companions. As night draws in, they fly back to their shared roosting place and spend the hours of darkness sleeping together. This long-term togetherness may have the advantage of enabling parrots to capitalize upon sporadically occurring conditions conducive to nesting. When these arise, no time is wasted looking for a mate; parrots simply get on with the business of breeding, sometimes without any great ceremony apart from courtship feeding and copulation.

Marked sexual differences tend to be found in polygamous birds (eg pheasants), or in those in which the males form only brief bonds with members of the opposite sex (eg birds of paradise and manakins). In these cases, resplendent plumage has evolved for impressing both hens and rival cocks during their fleeting sexual encounters. Strong dimorphism has also developed in birds that breed rapidly in response to sudden gluts of food; weaver birds, for instance, become imbued with a sense of urgency after rain has triggered the growth of seed-bearing grasses. Parrot partners that stay together year in, year out, have no need of special sexual recognition marks. Also, nesting inside hollow trees the hens, unlike ducks, have not 'needed' to evolve dingy camouflaged plumage for concealment during the incubation period. However, in a few parrots the sexes are markedly different from each other.

In the New World, fourteen kinds of parrotlets display a modest degree of sexual dimorphism. These live in semi-arid areas, and exist chiefly on grass seeds rather than on the fleshy pericarps of figs and berries. Two amazons also show sexual differences – the yellow-lored and white-fronted. In the latter species, the cock possesses bright-red wing coverts while the hen sports green. This bird lives on the dry lowlands of Mexico where the rainfall is fickle.

In lovebirds, sex is geared to the rains which bring a flush of food. Cocks and hens differ significantly from each other. These little parrots move around in flocks, and it is thought that in the wild the pair bonds disrupt after nesting. Obvious sexual signalling may therefore help to forge fresh pair bonds when conditions are favourable for breeding. But there may be another reason for such courtship. The hens appear to hold the upper rein and so the cock's wooing may reverse the dominance table, turning him into a forceful husband and her into a servile wife, thus enabling copulation to take place.

In Australia, the 'broad-tailed' parrots – a group that includes the rosellas, grass and *Psephotus* parakeets – are belligerent birds, with a marked antipathy towards body contact. Between the sexes, touching is virtually limited to fighting and mating; they are so aggressive towards others of their kind during the breeding season that, in captivity, the pairs must be isolated if they are to stand a chance of successful nesting. One-third of the species are sexually dimorphic, and this may be correlated with their nomadic habits and their need to respond to infrequent and unpredictable rainfall over much of their range.

The budgerigar is an exception. It lives in flocks, mainly in the interior of Australia where rainfall is usually sporadic. The birds must

A feeding scrummage of rainbow lorikeets at Currumbin Wildlife Sanctuary, Queensland, Australia (Jean-Paul Ferrero/Ardea London Ltd)

therefore be primed to nest at any time of year. Although the sexes have similar plumage, the cock reveals his gender by the blue of his cere and legs; the hen's are pinkish brown. The necklace of black spots across the throat is shown off by courting cocks, and there is evidence that the hens are drawn to individuals with the most prominent markings – the bigger the spots, the better. In other grass parakeets, too, there is a marked degree of sexual dimorphism; the scarlet chested hen, for instance, lacks her mate's red blaze. In the hooded, golden-shouldered, mulga and the red-rumped parakeets – all *Psephotus* parrots – the hens are modestly coloured in comparison to their flamboyantly hued mates.

Among the cockatoos, sexual dimorphism is restricted to the gang-gang and the bevy of blacks, the hens of which show a freckling or spotting on their plumage; in the red-tailed black, the hen lacks the magnificent crest of glossy feathers. However, in the galah, white, and sulphur-crested cockatoos, sex is revealed in the colour of the

Sulphur-crested cockatoo adopting a 'rain-bathing' posture in New Guinea (Alan Root/Bruce Coleman Ltd)

Scarlet and red and green macaws gathering to eat 'clay' at Manu National Park, Peru (Gunter Ziesler/Bruce Coleman Ltd)

eyes; the cocks have black eyes while the hens possess brown ones. Sexual differences also occur in cockatiels, pygmy and fig parrots.

By far the most exaggerated sexual differentiation is exhibited by the eclectus, a squat parrot that lives in Papua New Guinea and in the Cape York peninsula of Australia. The hens are overwhelmingly vermilion with a broad purple band across their bellies, while the cocks are basically green with red underwing coverts. Even the bills and irises differ between the sexes; the hen possesses yellowish white eyes and a black beak, while her partner has red eyes and a coral-coloured upper mandible. No one knows the significance of these differences. The birds live in tropical forest and on more open savannah countryside dotted with clumps of trees where they occasionally assemble in quite large flocks to feed and roost. Reproductive activities take place throughout the year. Groups of eclectus parrots breed in traditional nesting trees, each hole being used in turn by a succession of hens. There is even a suspicion that in the wild these parrots may be cooperative breeders, dominant pairs being assisted perhaps by offspring from previous nests or by related adults. If this turns out to be true, the eclectus will be unique among parrots. However, there is a further mystery to be solved; cock birds are observed more frequently than hens. Are they really less common or are they perhaps more timid because of their conspicuous plumage?

Courtship, for most parrots, does not always involve sudden and dramatic changes of personality. The birds may already be well acquainted and, through clumping and allopreening, be firmly bonded. Parrots with sex on their minds go courting by performing a variety of fairly simple movements such as bowing, head pumping, hopping, wing flicking and flapping, tail wagging and pompous strutting. These activities look all the more impressive because they serve to flaunt the cock's poster-coloured plumage to good effect. Rainbow lorikeets have a large repertoire of displays, thirty of which have been described by James Serpell who studied these pugnacious birds in Australia. Many take the form of stylized locomotory and grooming movements strung together to form elaborate dances. Whether deeply bowing, head bobbing or wing fluttering, the rituals tend to show off one or other of the lorikeet's brilliant colour patterns. Many of these postures are used for intimidating rivals of the same species in highly competitive feeding situations, but the cocks also harness the displays for exciting and delighting the hens during the nesting season.

Passionately aroused males tend to raise their head feathers, and this action is particularly spectacular in cockatoos with their multicoloured 'fans'. The male palm cockatoo uses his perch like a trapeze, pivoting forwards and hanging upside down; he then opens his wings, spreads his tail and erects his wonderful crest. His blushing red cheeks also betray his emotional state. Blood also rushes to the face of macaws in such circumstances. Many parrots have coloured eyes; for example, king parrots have pale yellow ones, whereas in rainbow lorikeets they are bright orange. During sexual excitement, the irides constrict and cause the eyes to 'blaze'. This brings lustful gleams to the eyes of expectant cock parrots.

The objective of courtship is copulation. If the male's advances are sufficiently seductive, and the female's physiological condition is right, she solicits by crouching over the perch with her wings and tail raised. The way in which the cocks mount differs between Old World and New World species. In the former, the amorous parrot steps onto his mate's back with both feet, whereas in the latter species the male retains one foot for holding onto the perch. Budgerigars have developed a further refinement because, for a second or two, the cock drapes his wing over the female's shoulder while his vent is brought close to hers for the transference of sperm. This is achieved by 'cloacal kissing'. The male's tail is lowered to one side, and the cloaca makes contact with the mate's during the course of twisting and thrusting movements. Copulation lasts for up to 90 seconds for both budgerigars and galahs, but, true to their name, lovebirds keep this activity up for 6 minutes. The proceedings are usually brought to an abrupt ending by the female threatening the male over her shoulder.

One might not rate the parrot's voice as an instrument of seduction, although some can produce quite mellifluous calls. One vocalisation uttered by the eclectus parrot has a rather lovely bell-like quality, and the red-rumped parrot, a common species from southern Australia, produces an agreeable trill which is as near as any member of the family comes to making avian music. And yet there is evidence that

Display used by Palm
Cockatoo in trees in
which they congregate

voice does play a part in the arousal of parrot passion. Hen budgerigars, for instance, need to hear the chatter of the cocks to bring them into breeding fettle. The call in question is the loud warble typically performed by males showing off their yellow crown and spotted throat feathers. Budgie crooning may go on for bouts of 4 minutes and account for 40 minutes out of every hour. Even hens kept in total darkness will come into full ovarian activity providing they can hear the cocks' rapturous chatter. Orange-chinned parakeets from South America perform duets when the members of a pair are in a highly excited state. Each produces a series of distinctive, melodious chirps, the higher pitched calls coming from the male, the lower ones from his mate; but integrated so nicely that the vocalisation appears to come from one individual. Such rapidly alternating sequences of calls exchanged between partners probably helps to coordinate the behaviour of the pair. Sound is certainly crucial to the sex life of New Zealand's kakapo.

SEX AND THE GROUNDED PARROT

The kakapo is a 'lek' breeder and, like all birds with this arrangement for courting, like the black grouse, is a specialist in the brief encounter. The cocks gather at a traditional site where they defend small territories and display vigorously. Females drop in, inspect the talent on offer, mate with the dominant cock, and then leave to raise one-parent families. As only a few of the most desirable cocks perform most of the mating, the system is a form of polygamy. Birds from nine different families have evolved lekking behaviour, and there are examples from the insects, fish, amphibians and mammals. In the kakapo's case, the cocks may be no closer than 50m (165ft) to each other, but they are still in a position to compete vocally.

The 'stage' for the male's courtship is a scrape around which the vegetation has been meticulously cleared. The birds dig a number of scrapes connected by well worn tracks through the undergrowth. These bowls are often placed in such a way in relation to nearby trees or rock faces as to act like sound reflectors, each bird establishing a series of these on a ridge or a hill top. The birds are in season from late

Male Kakapo displaying to its mate

November to early January, remaining for perhaps six hours or more nightly putting on a display of rocking and wing flapping. But the *pièce de résistance* of the performance is the deep booming, likened to the sound made by blowing across the opening of a bottle. The noise is surprisingly powerful because it carries for nearly 5km (3 miles), like a fog horn, across the dank forest. The bird first inflates its chest to gross proportions before emitting three or four quiet grunts. Then the kakapo's voice gets underway and the grunts gradually build up into an impressive crescendo of loud booms at 2 sec intervals. A minute or so later, the bird starts singing all over again. Such performances can go on all night, the male emitting perhaps 17,000 booms; sometimes the session lasts for 17 hours during gloomy weather. Unfortunately, the calls were partly the kakapo's downfall. Although designed to lure mates, the booms drew the attention of human hunters in days past, and was one of the factors that led to the birds' near total demise.

The kakapo's behaviour is especially interesting because it was thought that these communal courtship systems were evolved on the basis of safety in numbers, protecting the creatures preoccupied by sex. However, the kakapo's lekking arose in New Zealand long before mammalian predators appeared on the scene. The circumstances that favoured this arrangement remain a mystery.

PARROTS AT HOME

Although galahs and sulphur-crested cockatoos tend to occupy their nest holes all the year round, most parrots need to house-hunt afresh each season. Vacant cavities high up in dead or decaying trees provide most of them with ideal homes beyond the reach of ground-based predators. The holes must be more or less ready for occupation because, despite their formidable beaks, most parrots have not mastered the skills of excavating chambers like woodpeckers. In the main, parrots rely upon fire and lightning to damage trees and leave them open to attack by agents of the rotten world about us. Termites, with their ability to digest cellulose, and fungi, often eat away the insides of trees which then become settled by parrots and other cavity-nesting creatures. In Australia, the eucalypts are tailor-made for these birds, because they tend to shed branches, and the activities of tree-nesting termites produce a wealth of hollow limbs and trunks even in vigorously growing specimens. If the cavity approximately meets the needs of the new occupants, they sometimes set to work and idly chisel away at the entrance or the bowl inside. A chewed hole is a sure sign of occupancy by rosellas. The yellow-tailed black, glossy, and palm cockatoos may spend three months nibbling and chewing at the interiors, producing up to 0.3m (14in) depth of soft chippings on which the eggs will eventually be laid. Fig parrots actually excavate their own nests and work as a team in removing the soft fibrous wood; the hen scrapes while her partner turfs the dross out into the open.

Unfortunately, this reliance upon decaying limbs of forest trees is a disadvantage in areas where ageing woodlands have been destroyed or replaced by plantations of young trees. Unable to hew out and fashion their own living quarters, parrots are finding themselves increasingly without homes unless nest boxes are erected by benevolent land-

Galah feeding young in tree trunk nesting hole

owners. The shortage of nest cavities is certainly critical for cockatoos in parts of Australia where land has been cleared for agriculture or for reafforestation with fast growing conifers. In these areas, it is not unusual for a hole to be used in relays by several pairs of parrots.

Parrots tend to choose sites at a considerable height in the canopies of trees. Macaws nest 40m (130ft) up in palm trees; the cavities are often open to the sky and this lays the occupants open to a drenching when it rains. Three pairs of eclectus parrots which nested in a mature fig tree in the Iron Range of Australia had entrances 22, 28 and 58m (72, 92, 190ft) above the ground. However, occasionally the tunnel leading to the nest chamber is very long. Although crimson rosellas and king parrots select cavities with entrances 10m (30ft) above the ground, the nests themselves are virtually at foot level because of the long vertical descent inside the trunk. Mulga and turquoise parakeets, on the other hand, sometimes abandon their traditional nesting locations and choose to rear their families fairly low down in rotten fence posts. Some species actually nest on the ground or beneath it. Both the kea and kakapo are ground nesters, the latter choosing cavities beneath the roots of trees or in crevices between rocks. In Australia, three small parrots raise their families at ground level. The ground parrot places its nest in a depression sheltered by clumps of grass or bushes; tussocks of spinnifex are favoured by the night parrot, which creates a passage to the centre of the plant and builds its nest on a platform 20-30cm (8-12in) above the ground; the rock parrot tends to nest beneath overhanging slabs of stone, sometimes just above high-tide level. In South America, several species go underground. Best known is the Patagonian conure, a splendid slate-brown bird splashed with red and yellow. These birds nest colonially in cliffs and river banks in Chile and Argentina. The pairs burrow into soft lime and sandstone for 3m (10ft), then excavate a nest chamber about 40cm (15in) long and 15cm (6in) high. In large colonies, the ground is riddled by their tunnels, many of which run into each other.

Parrots vary in their need for space. Some, like the broad-tailed parrots and Major Mitchell's cockatoo are fiercely territorial and will not tolerate others of the same kind nesting nearby. Pairs of Major Mitchell's cockatoos nest kilometres apart whereas galahs and budgerigars are limited only by the density of the available nest sites; several pairs may set up home in one tree. In Peru's Manu National Park, a 'grove' of dead trees may attract several pairs of prospecting macaws, but only one or two will nest in each square mile and a half of forest. Proper social nesting has only evolved in the Patagonian conure, the African lovebirds and the South American monk parakeet; these include the master builders of the parrot world.

PARROTS AS BUILDERS

All lovebirds are unusual insofar as they construct nests inside pre-existing cavities. Those of the Madagascan, Abyssinian and red-faced lovebirds are comparatively simple, consisting of soft material deposited on the floor. However, the more advanced white-eye-ringed species make more complex nests, consisting of a tunnel terminating in a roofed chamber. The hens do all the work, using their sharp beaks

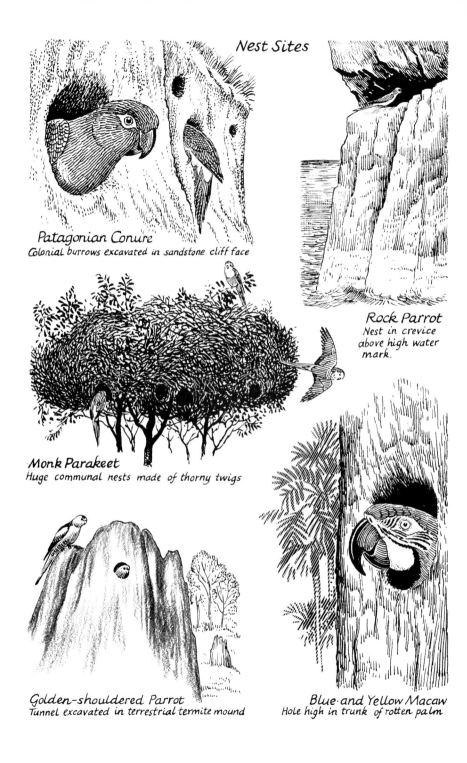

Nest Sites

Patagonian Conure
Colonial burrows excavated in sandstone cliff face

Rock Parrot
Nest in crevice above high water mark.

Monk Parakeet
Huge communal nests made of thorny twigs

Golden-shouldered Parrot
Tunnel excavated in terrestrial termite mound

Blue-and-Yellow Macaw
Hole high in trunk of rotten palm

to cut pliable material such as leaves and bark into strips. These are then carried to the nest site in a most unusual manner – at least by some of the lovebirds. In those with white eye-rings – Fischer's, the black-masked, the Nyasaland, and black-cheeked – the hens transport the building material in their beaks, as do most birds. However, the primitive species carry their payloads in their plumage, a habit they share only with the hanging parakeets to which they are related. In the Madagascan, Abyssinian and red-faced lovebirds, the hens tuck 6-8 small pieces of material among their erected body feathers. Once inserted, the plumage is sleeked to keep a grip on the stowed strips of vegetation while it is flown back to the nest site. Peach-faced lovebirds cut longer pieces, enabling them to build more complicated woven nests. Fabric of this length can only be stowed between the relatively large feathers of the rump and lower back. Even so, the birds often lose half their cargo in flight, whereas those species that carry the stuff in their beaks waste very little.

Experiments conducted nearly thirty years ago by William C. Dilger at the Laboratory of Ornithology, Ithaca, New York, revealed that the behaviour has a genetic basis. Lovebirds hybridize fairly easily in captivity, so he crossed peach-faced with Fischer's lovebirds and discovered that the offspring were initially very 'mixed up' when they came to build nests themselves. Inheriting behaviour patterns from both their parents, they could not decide whether to carry the pieces of nest-building material in their beaks or whether to tuck them into their rump feathers. Sometimes they managed to carry the bits in their beaks, but strips of bark in their plumage generally fell out because they did not firmly sleek their feathers before flying. After several months, they learned to forsake the abortive but innate tucking in favour of the beak-carrying method typical of Fischer's lovebird.

The origin of this unique method of transporting nest material may be due to the fortuitous juxtaposition of two unrelated pieces of behaviour – beak honing and preening. During idle moments, parrots tend to chew bits of wood or bark to keep their beaks sharp, and sometimes this behaviour leads directly to feather erection and preening. When this happens, parrots occasionally deposit whatever they have been nibbling between the ruffled feathers and accidentally leave the

Peach-faced Lovebird collecting nest materials and placing them in back plumage for carrying to nest site.

material *in situ*. Such chance behaviours are the very raw material of evolution and, in the case of the lovebirds and hanging parakeets, initiated the development of this unusual nesting behaviour.

The most spectacular nests in the parrot world are built by monk parakeets. These gregarious green and grey birds range across Bolivia, southern Brazil and Argentina, where they live in flocks of up to a hundred individuals along water courses and in savannah woodland. They are unique among parrots because of the manipulative skills which enable them to make proper, free-standing nests of outstanding size. These bulky stacks of dry, thorny sticks are placed in the topmost branches of trees. Although lone pairs occasionally set up home by themselves, several pairs usually contribute to the structures, each having its own separate entrance pointing obliquely downwards, thus making it very awkward for enemies to gain access to the brood. Some nests are composed of 20 or so breeding chambers; W. H. Hudson, on his travels in Argentina early this century, found one that tipped the scales at 200kg (440lb). Another nest, occupied by only 5 pairs of parakeets, measured 2m (6½ft) from top to bottom. Such nests are probably built over the course of several years; the birds use them all year round for roosting as well as breeding, and fresh pairs add to the existing structure. In the end, the well established ones are so broad and strong that they are occasionally settled by jabiru storks, tree ducks and caracaras.

PARROTS AS LODGERS

Other birds sometimes provide parrots with ready made nests. Many a woodpecker has been heaved out of its hole by a pair of house-hunting parrots. Pacific parrotlets have been recorded moving into the great stick nests of necklaced spine tails, and tiny blue-winged parrotlets commandeer the mud domes of oven birds, which they line with grass stems. In Africa, masked lovebirds sometimes use the old nests of swifts, whereas groups of peach-faced lovebirds often take up residence in the communal nests of social weavers. The pairs invade the haystack-like structures and supplant some of the rightful owners in their nesting chambers. However, red-faced lovebirds from West and Central Africa turn to termites to provide them with favourable breeding sites, excavating their nests in arboreal castles of clay constructed by these social insects. Several other parrots also lodge in termitaria.

Fifty or so kinds of birds breed inside either terrestrial or arboreal nests of termites. They include 23 species of kingfishers (a quarter of the family!), 4 trogons, a couple of kinds of puff-birds, a jacamar, and a cotinga. Among the parrots, 13 (4 per cent) carve their breeding cavities in the hard, black material manufactured by termites. Apart from the fact that the agglutinated faeces and wood debris used for constructing the outside walls of the edifices set like concrete, the interior of the nests are 'air conditioned' and maintain a fairly constant temperature. However, once the walls are breached, the termites quickly set to work repairing the damage. Once the birds have finished digging out their quarters in the more friable inner part of the nest, the insects seal the exposed ends of their galleries, and so there is then no further contact between the termites and their uninvited guests. The birds continue to benefit from the warmth and shelter afforded by the reinforced construction.

The association may have arisen because many of the cavities that parrots nest in are created by termite activity in the first place. Indeed, red-faced lovebirds burrow into termitaria already located in the trunks of trees; aviculturists simulate the situation for their captive ones by filling up nest boxes with clay to encourage them to dig and breed. Only the hens have the expertise to excavate, their mates' attempts are usually counter-productive. All the pygmy parrots burrow into termitaria projecting like great cankers from the sides of tropical trees. Several South American parakeets (eg, orange-fronted, yellow-winged and blue-winged) have been observed using these structures, although they all breed in more orthodox locations as well.

One Australian species, the golden-shouldered parakeet, appears to nest nowhere else. It and the possibly extinct paradise parakeet choose terrestrial termite mounds a few feet in height. The paradise parakeet's entrance is 3cm (1in) in diameter and 23cm (9in) long, and leads to a circular chamber 36cm (14in) in diameter. C. H. H. Jerrard, a Queensland naturalist, was one of the last to watch these birds breeding in the Upper Burnett River valley, and in 1921 he took poignant photographs of the birds and their nest site. The golden-shouldered, an equally pretty little parakeet, still survives. These usually breed in spire-shaped mounds, but occasionally select 'magnetic' or meridian termitaria; these constructions are very flattened and oriented north-south so that the broad sides of the nests catch the warmth of the early morning and late afternoon sun while avoiding the searing solar radiation around the middle of the day. The parakeets inside their compartment probably profit from this management of solar heat. This particular species hosts its own nest lodgers. Inside the nesting chamber live the larvae of a scavenging moth. The grubs presumably exist on the excrement voided by the young parakeets.

PARROTS ON EGGS

As the time approaches for the hens to lay eggs, their requirement for extra food is met by an increased frequency of courtship feeding. Male macaws at this stage of the reproductive cycle go around with greatly distended throat pouches in which is stored food for their mates. The activity may help to stimulate the hens into breeding condition. Feeding is by regurgitation, the cock transferring to his mate partly digested food from his crop. For most of the year, this extra nourishment may be of no great consequence, apart from its symbolic importance in maintaining the pair bond. However, at the onset of the nesting season, the extra resources may contribute towards the formation of the eggs. Once the hen settles down to brood, she makes only brief forays into the open air, so the cock's continued offerings must sustain her for several weeks.

Like so many cavity-nesting birds, parrots produce white eggs. There are two explanations. Firstly, very pale eggs show up best in dim surroundings, so white ones are easy to locate at the bottom of a gloomy hole. However, the nature of the parrot's protected site may have obviated the need for camouflage; without the evolutionary pressure for colour matching and disruptive patterns, hen parrots may have simply lost the ability to lay 'pretty' eggs.

For their size, parrots lay relatively small eggs. At 8.4cm (3¼in) the buff-faced pygmy parrot is the tiniest member of the family, and lays eggs the size of cherry stones. The bigger the parrot, the smaller its

Cock White-fronted Amazon courtship feeding his mate

eggs, relatively speaking. The magnificent green-winged macaw almost 1m (3ft) long, produces elliptical ones measuring only 5cm x 3.5cm (2 x 1½in), which are barely larger than those laid by lapwings. The comparatively puny size of parrot's eggs is correlated with the developmental state of the chicks when they emerge. Birds which lay relatively bulky eggs usually have young which must fend for themselves the moment they break out of the shell like waders, wildfowl and pheasants. Parrots rear their chicks in protected nests, and lavish upon them much care and attention; the nestlings accordingly hatch in a less advanced state of development.

Parrots fall broadly into two types depending upon the level of investment in each of their offspring. Some parrots tend to produce big families in the hope that a few of their young will reach maturity. They produce large clutches and have comparatively short incubation and nestling periods. These parrots are often nomadic, existing on protein-rich herbaceous seeds, and often breed precipitately in response to sudden rainfall. The grass parakeets (including budgerigars) and lovebirds fall into this category. On the other hand, the majority of parrots, especially the medium-sized and super-parrots, produce few young but invest much time in rearing them. These species specialize on a fruit, nectar or pollen diet, have small clutches (1-3 eggs), the hens incubate them for a relatively long period, and they have an extended phase of rearing the nestlings. Macaws, amazons, lories and lorikeets belong to this group.

The clutch size reveals the quality of parental investment. The glossy cockatoo is an exceptional parrot because the hens only produce 1 egg during the breeding season. The minimum clutch is usually 2 (eg the macaws and black cockatoos); inland red-tailed black cockatoos may sometimes nest at 6-month intervals in south-west Australia. The budgerigar occasionally lays as many as 8 eggs before completing the clutch, thus rivalling the tits for productivity. These eggs are generally laid at 2-day intervals and, with the exception of the cockatoos and cockatiel, are incubated solely by the hen, although her mate may spend some time in the nest keeping her company.

In lovebirds, the hens lay from 3 to 8 eggs over the course of 1-2 weeks, and each needs to be incubated for 23 days before hatching. As the hen becomes broody immediately after the first egg appears, there is considerable disparity in the size of the nestlings by the time the last egg pips. The smaller chicks are at a competitive disadvantage in securing the parents' attention. They only survive when the supply of food is good; in lean times they die. Although to us it seems a cruel arrangement, staggered hatching is a good system for matching breeding productivity with the level of resources. Budgerigars and other small parakeets are also opportunistic nesters and lay comparatively large clutches when there is plenty of food around. These vary from 4 to 8 eggs depending on whether the countryside is verdant or not. The hen commences sitting after the second egg appears, and they hatch after 18 days.

Hen macaws sit for a month on their 2-egg clutches before the shells start to chip. In Australian black cockatoos, the second egg rarely results in a successfully fledged youngster unless the food supply is especially prolific. The 'white' and 'pink' cockatoos tend to lay rather larger clutches and take less time to hatch them. Galahs in south-west Australia studied by Ian Rowley of the Commonwealth Scientific and Industrial Research Organisation (CSIRO) lay clutches of 4, the eggs being produced at intervals of 2 or 3 days and taking 23.4 days to hatch. As in all cockatoos, the sexes share the task of incubation, and start seriously to sit after the fourth egg is laid, resulting in staggered hatching. During the day, the partners relieve each other at the nest about every hour, although which one keeps the clutch warm at night when both birds are roosting in the nest chamber remains a mystery.

PARROTS AS PARENTS

When a parrot emerges into the world, its looks belie the beautiful creature that it will turn into. The squirming little pink creature is more often than not naked, blind and, in the case of the New World species, without any external ear opening, at least until the eyes open. A brand new parrot has been likened to an avian version of E.T., especially baby cockatoos which have a lump on their crown from which the crest quills emerge. And yet as soon as they are dry, they express their hunger by head bobbing and clamouring for food. To help them, the chicks of New World parrots possess swellings or 'nodes' at the base of their mandibles which persist for several weeks after the birds have flown the nest. These are particularly well formed in the macaws and conures. Their chicks beg strongly in response to pressure exerted on the nodes. It is thought that these knobs enable the parents to obtain a good grip on the nestlings' beaks when regurgitating food, especially when the chicks are getting large and boisterous. However, why all young parrots are not so equipped, remains a puzzle.

At first, the baby parrots are offered soft food by their mother. The material is made all the more digestible because it is twice pre-processed, initially by the cock who passed it from his crop to the hen, who in turn continued to digest it before transferring some into the tiny gape of the nestling. She accomplishes this by taking its beak in hers and pumping the mash into its gullet. For several days, the chicks are given their sustenance by this route, the advantage being that the food will be well softened and easily assimilated by the growing birds. As the chicks increase in stature, the parents individually seek food and offer this directly to the ever ravenous brood. With age, their digestive systems can cope with tougher material, and in the end, the graminivorous species may place barely hulled seeds in their youngsters' beaks. The budgerigar, however, is an exceptional parrot insofar as the newly hatched chicks are given something akin to milk.

Very few birds are able to manufacture what seems to be a characteristic mammalian product. In pigeons of both sexes, the crop secretes the protein and fat-rich fluid to sustain the squabs for the first few days of their lives. Even more remarkable is the cock emperor penguin which produces milk from its oesophagus so that, after forty days of incubation, he can greet his chick with a rich 'beverage' upon which it will double its weight before the hen returns with krill. Greater flamingos do not regurgitate pre-digested food for their young, but feed them for up to a month on milk enriched with blood, each parent yielding 100ml (3.5fl oz) a day. Hen budgerigars produce milk in their oesophagus. It is very rich in protein, and essential in giving the newly hatched chicks a good start in life. To begin with, the soft, creamy substance is crammed into the little creature's crop, but after a time the diet is supplemented by crushed and partly digested seeds. So far, this is the only parrot known to make 'crop' milk.

Even before their eyes open, young parrots show a strong sense of togetherness. Budgerigars and lovebirds, for instance, huddle in a heap with each chick interlocking its neck over the individual beneath it. The oldest and dominant youngster tends to sit on top of the stack and the smallest is at the bottom. This may serve to keep the little animals warm at a time when they are not well clothed with feathers. However, once the eyes open, the orientation of the chicks inside the nest chamber becomes more random.

Budgerigars are specialists in rapid reproduction. When the chicks are 9-10 days old, their bodies are covered with greyish down, and the wing quills are already visible. The eyes open after another day, and by the time they are 3 weeks old, the bodies are fully feathered. However, the young birds do not take their first flight until about their 36th day, and do not become fully independent of their parents for a further 2 weeks. As young parrots are quite safe in their nurseries, there has not been evolutionary pressure for early fledging as has been the case with many birds which rear their young in open nests. Even the relatively small lovebirds take about 43 days to leave their holes; rainbow lorikeets and lories fledge when they are between 7 and 8 weeks old; thick-billed and African grey parrots take 60 and 70 days respectively; but young macaws probably do not leave their nest cavity until they are 3 months old, and are probably supported by their parents for considerably longer.

Detailed knowledge of the family life of wild macaws is beginning to emerge from Charles Munn's studies in the Manu National Park in Peru. The large macaws do not seem to be prolific breeders even in the pristine virgin forest of Manu where conditions are as ideal for them as anywhere else in South America. Individual pairs may not nest every year, something that probably holds good for some of the cockatoos and amazons. Furthermore, of those that do nest, the proportion that successfully produce young may be small. Of 20 nests of scarlet, and blue and yellow macaws that Munn was monitoring, no less than 7 failed; sometimes the failure rate may be as high as 50 per cent due to flooding and predators which enter the holes and devour the brood. Competition for cavities with bees and other birds may be another cause of unsuccessful breeding. Sometimes other macaws are the rivals; Munn recorded a prospecting couple of blue and yellow macaws intimidating a nesting pair with two offspring in their tree cavity. The breeding male eventually disappeared – Munn discovered some macaw remains at the bottom of the tree – and the female tried valiantly to maintain her family. However, one of the interlopers finally entered the nest while the mother was foraging and turfed out one of the youngsters which fell to the ground, thus effectively killing it. The remaining bird left the nest early. With all these problems to put up with, Munn estimates that 100 pairs of macaws are unlikely to rear more than 15-25 offspring annually. Observations of macaws on their daily rounds provided the information. The majority of sightings were of couples – like most parrots, macaws do everything with their mate. However, 10-15 per cent of the observations referred to trios, and a further 5-10 per cent to quartets of birds. These seemed to be mature pairs and their full grown offspring, which indicated that the young macaws may consort with their parents for many months after they have left the nest. Further information on breeding success comes from studies of cockatoos in Western Australia.

Young galahs are brooded by both parents for the first 10 days of life; the offspring are constantly attended during morning, evenings and night, but intermittently during the afternoon when it is warm. Both parents regurgitate food in response to the clamour of their offspring, returning to the nest with distended crops approximately every 106 minutes. Fledging takes place in succession as each youngster reaches 50 days of age. The breeding productivity varies from year to year, but over the course of a 7-year period, the average percentage of young galahs that left the nest was 59. As 32 per cent of the broods failed completely, the successful ones fledged 84 per cent of the nestlings that hatched. Several causes of failure were identified; occasionally the nest with its contents was simply deserted; another problem was driving rain and subsequent flooding that chilled the eggs; there was also an unidentifiable disease that afflicted and killed a variable number of nestlings each year. Ian Rowley's programme of research revealed that a pair of breeding galahs might rear on average 2 (1.9) young each year – a figure that compares with 1.6 per pair for corellas, and about 1 per pair for white cockatoos. However, as shooting inflicts a considerable mortality on young galahs, a pair of adults may need as many as eight breeding seasons to replace themselves.

Galahs are unusual parrots because the fledglings join nursery groups or crèches, watched over by a few adults, after they have quit their nesting holes. Like all parrot parents, the galahs encourage their young to make their maiden flights by calling them out of the nest. When the youngsters make their inaugural flight, they can fly as strongly as their parents, but have some difficulty in making accomplished turns and landings. These skills are practised and perfected in the crèches. The young galah usually makes its way to one on its first flight, perhaps located in the top of a stand of trees several kilometres from its home. Here young galahs from the neighbourhood gather, practising acrobatics on the branches, learning to manoeuvre in the air, grooming and calling for attention from their parents. Once all the fledglings have assembled in the crèche, the birds fly as families to local feeding spots where the parents continue for a time to provide for their brood. When they are about three months old, the difficult time arrives when their parents desert them, and they must then range over the countryside with many other birds of their year in juvenile mobs. Like all cockatoos, they will not assume the responsibilities of parenthood until they are perhaps three years old.

Young parrots may have a lot to learn in order to survive. For immature macaws, making a living in the canopy of the rainforest must be a daunting prospect, knowing which plants are poisonous, the location of the best food trees and how to deal effectively with the fruit and nuts. Young primates are faced with many of the same problems, and they benefit from the wisdom of their elders by associating with them in family groups. This echoes the family arrangements of macaws. There is another parallel between parrots and primates; both 'play'. Parrots are highly exploratory creatures and often engage in activities which seem to have no other purpose except pleasure. How else can one interpret the activities of kea lying on their backs and sliding down the roofs of alpine huts in the New Zealand alps!

There is evidence that yellow-tailed black cockatoos learn to excavate grubs from deep inside wood. If pieces of wood containing the noisily chewing larvae of cossid moths are given to a young, naïve bird, it fails to react to them. However, an adult immediately sets to work and devours the fat morsels. Parrots are undeniably 'smart' birds, and it does not stretch one's credulity too far to think that these birds are capable of watching others and copying their behaviour – parrot culture! The extent to which parrots are able to modify their behaviour in the wild is revealed by cuckoo cockatoos.

CUCKOO COCKATOOS

Occasionally cross-fostering happens in the wild. In Australia, galahs and Major Mitchell's cockatoos infrequently lay claim to the same hole, the hens of both species beginning their clutches at the same time. In these mix-ups, the galahs invariably lose out to the larger and more pugnacious pink birds, but manage to bequeath an egg or two to the victor's clutch. Young galahs are therefore reared by the Major Mitchell's along with their own nestlings. When they fledge, the galahs, not surprisingly, identify with their foster parents, completely ignoring mobs of their own species. What is more, the cuckoo-cockatoos behave like Major Mitchell's cockatoos, selecting the same food, even modifying their wing beats to match those of their companions, as well as imitating their calls. However, when startled, the fostered birds 'forget themselves' and tend to lapse into pukka galah behaviour. But, when they reach sexual maturity, the 'imprinted' galahs opt for Major Mitchell's as partners, and occasionally manage to nest successfully, thus accounting for the occasional hybrids recorded in wild populations.

El Oro Parakeet

4 · PARROTS DISCOVERED

Parrots are still being discovered. On 4 August 1980, a party of North American scientists were surveying remnant patches of cloud forest west of Pinas in the Ecuador province of El Oro. On this western slope of the Andes, they observed a flock of nine smallish parakeets feeding in the canopy, which, at first, they took to be maroon-tailed parakeets, *Pyrrhura melanoleuca*. However, all the birds displayed splashes of scarlet on their forehead, and lacked the scaling on their breast. Could these belong to a species new to science? That question was not answered until 1985 when a joint expedition was launched under the auspices of the Academy of Natural Sciences, Philadelphia, and the Museo de Ciençias Nationales in Quito, Ecuador. The team spent three weeks in the area where the original birds were observed, discovered that the parakeets were relatively numerous in the fragments of forest, and estimated a local population of at least 55 to 60 occurring in flocks of between 4 and 12 individuals. A dozen were 'collected'. A year later, a field party returned to find the northern

95

limits of the bird's distribution, and a further 4 specimens were taken 100km (62 miles) north of the original locality. From an examination of the birds in the hand, it was quite clear that they belonged to a hitherto undescribed parrot, but one closely related to the maroon-tailed parakeet. A full description was eventually published in the *Wilson Bulletin* of June 1988 by Robert S. Ridgely and Mark B. Robbins who christened this, the 333rd species of parrot, the El Oro parakeet, *Pyrrhura orcesi*.

Although restricted to a narrow band of forest between 600 and 1,100m (1,970 and 3,610ft) in elevation over a range of 100km (62 miles), El Oro parakeets were not at the time extremely scarce, and yet these birds had successfully evaded detection until this decade. (The British Museum subsequently found a specimen in its huge collection of skins, but nobody had realised its significance.)

The discovery of parrots often goes hand in hand with epic stories of European adventurers and navigators who expanded the horizon of the known world between the fifteenth and eighteenth centuries. The descriptions they brought back of those far-off lands were often couched in terms of the strange animals and plants that made an impact on the travellers; gloriously coloured and noisy parrots were often foremost in their accounts, especially of Australia and South America. However, long before such places were part of the accepted geography of the planet, ring-necked parakeets were involved in the culture of India, and it was through contact with the people of this sub-continent that the first knowledge of parrots filtered into Europe.

PARROTS FROM THE ORIENT

From the dawn of human history, people have always been involved with animals, hunting wild creatures and domesticating them for food, muscle power or for some useful commodity like wool or leather; sometimes animals were tamed and brought into homes for companionship and amusement. Chickens, pigeons and geese were domesticated at least 4,000 years ago for their potential as providers of food. As we shall see in Chapter 7, parrots are eaten by tribal people.

However, parrots were best appreciated for their brilliant feathers and for their other endearing quality – their voice.

On first acquaintance, a parrot's vocalisation is hardly everyone's idea of entertainment. Even the most ardent devotee of these birds will admit that a lusty shriek from a parrot is sufficient to make the blood curdle. And yet their ability to imitate the human voice with varying degrees of perfection has, over the ages, made the parrot an agreeable pet. If taken from its nest early in life, a parrot becomes finger tame and, if allowed, sticks like a shadow to its human companion; with the minimum of training it will learn enough phrases in any language to entertain its owner and thus repay its keep. By the middle of the first millennium BC, chattering parrots were kept in captivity, probably in Africa and most certainly in Asia.

Parrots were first recorded in the countries where they lived as wild birds. India possessed a cultured civilisation, rich in folklore and religion, and a tradition of writing. There were also parakeets. In fact, the scientific name for the whole order, Psittaciformes, comes from the Orient, being derived via the Greek *psittakos* from an Indian word for parrot. The first ever reference to these birds is found in the oldest piece of Indian literature, the *Rigveda*. Written over 3,000 years ago, it contains a touching hymn to the awakening morning when parrots are entrusted with taking care of the moon's pallid colour which fades before the glare of the rising sun. Talking parrots are not mentioned in the *Rigveda*; however, when the uncanny talent of these birds was discovered they were then given central roles in plays, fables and poems written in various Indian languages over the course of the next thousand years.

In those ancient times, parrots and palaces went together. Princes greatly appreciated parakeets as feathered friends, and young men of the wealthy upper classes spent much time encouraging their avian companions to speak, at least if the lessons in the *Kama Sutra* were to be taken seriously. This famous old Indian textbook was essential reading for all who aspired to gain the fullest sensual and spiritual enjoyment, out of living and loving. The Hindu sex manual spelt out sixty-four practices that men had to master, one of which was to teach a parrot to talk.

But these birds were even more firmly connected with human sexuality. The parakeet was considered to be a bird of love, perhaps through a recognition of the 'affectionate' behaviour displayed by mated pairs, sitting in contact with each other, billing and grooming. Whatever the origins of the association, Kama, the Hindu God of Love, chose a parrot to ride upon or to pull his chariot, as did his consort, Rati, the Goddess of Lust and Pleasure. Many voluptuous sculptures testify further to the sexual connection. High-class prostitutes signalled their trade by carrying a parrot on their wrist, and this is recorded in several Indian bas-reliefs. But a parakeet could also be a force for moral rectitude. There is one well known story in the Sanskrit work, the *Shukasaptaki*, where a pet bird uses its power of speech to dissuade the wife of a merchant, who is always away on business, from visiting her lover. Night after night the parrot keeps the woman's adulterous inclinations in check by telling her beguiling stories until, after seventy days, her husband returns and all is well. These charming tales eventually spread beyond India's frontiers, and during the Middle Ages were known in Europe.

THE FIRST PARROTS IN EUROPE

News of parrots first broke in Europe when travellers returned from the Orient. The first scholar to do so was a Greek doctor, Ctesias, who wrote about India in 397BC. He gave a good description of a tame parrot – *bittakos* he called it – which fits that of a plum-headed parakeet. The bird spoke Indian and could be taught Greek though, as it happens, 'ring-necked' parakeets are not the most skilful of birds in reproducing human-like speech. It may well have been a gift given by an Indian prince to the Persian king Ataxerxes II in whose court Ctesias worked for a time. However, seventy years later, Europeans at home could have seen for themselves at first hand these wonder birds. In 327BC, Alexander the Great, King of Macedonia, marched his army eastwards into India, having defeated the Persian Empire. Here, he fought a fierce battle with the rajah, Porus. Afterwards, Alexander's men refused to go further, but before returning home along the Indus one of them, a sailor called Oneskritos, took some tame parakeets as souvenirs of the campaign. This is the first recorded importation of parrots into Europe. It was the start of a steady trade in Indian 'ring-necked' parakeets; with the burgeoning of commerce between the Orient and the Greek city states, parrots became sufficiently familiar for Aristotle, that most outstanding of observers and founder of natural science, to discuss them in his biological writings. By the second century BC, Hephaiston, a Greek artist, produced the first picture of a parrot in mosaic at Pergamon. The bird is probably an Alexandrine parakeet and is so accurately portrayed that the artist must have seen the species for himself.

Parakeets from the east continued to enter Europe when the Greek civilization gave way to the Roman Empire. In those days, a pretty parrot uttering a little Latin was a prestigious pet, and cost more than a slave. Accordingly, they were kept in a style consistent with their high price tag, in splendid cages of gold and silver, lavishly decorated

Alexandrine (left) and Plum-headed Parakeets

with tortoise-shell and ivory. Soon, parakeets were respectable members of Roman society, and everybody who was anybody, from the emperor down, possessed a parrot which was often flaunted sitting on its owner's arm like a miniature falcon while he strolled around the streets. There were even recognised parrot teachers who were organised into a formal profession. The ability to talk led to the demise of some birds because parrot tongues were considered an appropriate snack for those whose power of speech was lacking. By sympathetic magic, eloquence could be restored by eating the tongues of talking birds! That, however, was not the fate of a parakeet mourned by a friend of the poet Ovid, who wrote a long elegy to mark its passing. Such was the popularity of parakeets that they were pictured on mosaics, murals, silver bowls and clay lamps. They were also depicted in books, including Pliny's *Naturalis Historia*. As a recorder, Pliny was excessively credulous; he collated not only a great number of facts but

Roman mosaic showing a pair of parakeets pulling a cart from Hans Struden Papageien Einst und Jetzt

also fanciful tales from travellers so that his natural history book is less than reliable. Despite this, the compendium, yarns and all, was the standard source of reference for centuries to come. It formed the basis of the medieval Bestiaries. Eventually, the Renaissance ushered in a new breed of people who were imbued with a refreshing sense of enquiry, and saw for themselves how things were. But, until the sixteenth century, Pliny's work provided the foundation for all information about parrots in zoological books.

After the decline of the Roman Empire in the fourth and fifth centuries, parrots tended to disappear from the record and did not emerge until the Middle Ages when crusaders, ambassadors and itinerant merchants once again returned with birds from their travels. They were 'ring-necked' parakeets and, like the Romans before them, proud owners kept the birds in ornamental cages designed for showing off their pampered and privileged pets. They also became part of the juggler's kit, as shown in a sketch drawn by a French architect, Villard de Honnecourt, between 1230 and 1235. It illustrates a lady juggler with possibly an Alexandrine parakeet on her wrist, while a dog jumps up at her waist. And news of other kinds of parrot was on the way.

Lady juggler with, possibly, an Alexandrine parakeet on her wrist

101

During the thirteenth century, Marco Polo, the indefatigable Venetian explorer, reported seeing all manner of parrots including white ones on the southern coast of India. These were probably cockatoos traded by Malayan fishermen that had found their way west as cage birds. However, the first sulphur-crested cockatoo to reach Europe may well have been the bird given to the great German emperor, Frederick II of Hohenstaufen, a brilliant and enlightened monarch with a passion for birds in general and falconry in particular. This cockatoo would have come from South East Asia, perhaps through China.

There are a few intriguing references to parrots dating from the fourteenth century – a grotesque parrot is drawn on the Mappa Mundi, a world map of about 1300 formerly held in Hereford Cathedral but at the time of writing in the Tate Gallery, London, and Chaucer makes mention of the remarkable imitative powers of parrots in his *Canterbury Tales*.

One of the next members of the parrot family to appear in Europe was the African grey. In 1402, the French conquered the Canary Isles and reported the presence of these handsome grey parrots with red tails, but they were captive ones imported by the natives from West Africa. By the middle of the century, the Portuguese controlled 3,000km (1,865 miles) of the West African coast and so grey parrots and maybe other kinds drifted into Europe on ships returning from that part of the tropics. The grey parrot was a much more fluent 'linguist' than its smaller Asiatic cousins, but to the religiously minded people of medieval Europe, any parrot's miraculous power of speech placed it close to man in the ladder of creation, and therefore closer to God than other dumb creatures. Any talking parrot was therefore accorded special status by the Church, and these birds were so esteemed in the Vatican during the reign of Pope Martin V that a Keeper of Parrots (Cortiele de Papagalli) was appointed. One particularly pious parrot was bought by a Venetian cardinal for 100 gold pieces – a considerable fortune in those days. Nevertheless, the bird gave good value for money because it could recite the Lord's Prayer faultlessly. Such birds continued to change hands for handsome sums of money so that only the rich could possess these status symbols. By the middle of the fifteenth century, Italian seafarers observed Senegal parrots on their travels and, during the course of plying their trade in spices in Asia, saw brilliant red lories and white cockatoos 'as large as chickens' in the Moluccan Islands. The Venetian, Nicolo de Conti, reported on the parrots of Ceram, and provided sufficiently good descriptions for ornithological scholars to identify the species he remembered seeing – red and purple-naped lories and the lovely pink, salmon-crested cockatoo. Some of these birds must have found their way back to European ports because in 1496 the Mantuan artist, Andrea Mantegna, portrayed a white cockatoo in one of his paintings.

THE AGE OF DISCOVERY

At the end of the fifteenth century, there was an insatiable demand for spices – cinnamon, cloves and peppers – for preserving food and making it palatable. Until then, Venice had monopolised the lucrative trade, and her vast wealth and political power was derived from it. However, that situation was to change because both Spain and Portugal had ambitions to muscle in on the business. Both were formidable marine powers, and they became locked in competition to take over the sea routes to India and the Moluccan spice islands. However, what they needed were fresh and quicker routes, and so began a series of epic explorations beyond the edge of the known world to chart new ways to the Indies.

Bartolomeu Dias seized the initiative for Portugal in 1488 when he sailed around the southern tip of Africa and proved that it was possible to reach the Indian Ocean by an easterly route. In 1497, Vasco da Gama followed his course and reached India to establish a trading post at Calicut on the Malabar coast. Meanwhile, New World parrots had been discovered as a result of the Spanish thrust westwards.

In 1492, Christopher Columbus, a Genoese in the service of Spain, ventured out across the Atlantic with three small ships, searching for a passage to the East Indies. He must have been aware of the belief that 'where there are parrots, there is also gold' and, not surprisingly, captains of the Spanish Main were also eager to find evidence of these birds during the course of their explorations because of the promise of greater riches. Columbus did not have long to wait. Even before he sighted the Bahamas, a flock of parrots flying over the sea is supposed to have caused him to veer southwards and make landfall in the Caribbean. (In fact, the birds are most likely to have been shearwaters heading towards their nesting holes on land. Nevertheless the historical account refers to parrots.) Had Columbus continued on his original heading, he may well have gone down in history for having discovered Florida and the vast North American continent.

Once ashore on the Bahama Islands, and later on Cuba and Haiti, he saw parrots galore and so takes credit for being the first European to set his eyes upon American species. These were Cuban amazons, rather lovely birds, each with a white blaze on its forehead, a ruby throat and chest, and blue wings. They were exchanged by the native Indians for Columbus's own gifts, and when he returned to Spain the birds went with him, to be displayed to the reigning monarchs and to admiring crowds in Seville and Barcelona. The following year, Columbus embarked on another transatlantic voyage, and finally put ashore on Guadaloupe and Trinidad where he saw spectacular macaws which, at the time, occupied several of the islands in that part of the world. Three years later the Portuguese chanced upon Brazil, thus putting South America firmly on the map as a land brimming with parrots.

On 9 March 1500, Pedro Alvares Cabral led the first proper trading expedition to Calicut with 13 larger ships, caravels, 1,200 men, 8 Franciscan friars and 9 chaplains. Although his fleet was heading for Cape Verde on the first leg of its course, the north-east trade winds swept it to the coast of Brazil, on which he put ashore on 23 April. The haven Cabral found he named Porto Seguro, and all accounts of his ten-day stay indicate that his crew were as deeply impressed by the sight of the parrots as by anything else they witnessed. Among the birds were macaws which the naked but handsome natives referred to as *macauba*. Others were 'as large as hens', and trinkets were bartered for 'two very large and beautiful red parrots, and two little green ones'. Cabral ordered the fleet to head east towards the Indian Ocean, but

A rare orange-bellied parrot feeding its chicks in Tasmania (Dave Watts)

ran into tempestuous weather around the Cape of Good Hope which caused several of his ships to sink with all hands. The survivors refitted in Mozambique and headed back to Lisbon. The first to arrive was one of the small caravels, the *Anunciada,* which docked on 23 June 1501 with a cargo of spices and two marvellous parrots of 'more than an arm and a half in length'. These were probably scarlet macaws and the first of their kind to reach Europe. One can only imagine how people reacted to these living palettes of glorious colour.

The Venetians, however, were deeply worried by the threat to their economy caused by such valuable cargoes arriving in Lisbon, being warned in a dispatch sent by their ambassador to the Doge of Venice. Among other things, it reported that above the Cape of Good Hope, towards the west, the Portuguese had discovered a new land – 'They call it that of parrots...' The dispatch was published and so, reinforced by the knowledge of the avian riches plundered from that part of the world, the land became popularly known as Terra de Papagaios (Land of Parrots). It was accordingly identified by cartographers well into the sixteenth century by representations of macaws and red dyewood trees called *brasilia* that were widespread in that country. Before the name Brazil became established, the country was referred to as Bresilia sive Terra Papagalli (Brazil or Land of the Parrot).

Everywhere the conquistadors marched, they discovered parrots of all shapes and sizes, some like sparrows, others as big as pheasants. They also found tame ones in the villages and camps of the local inhabitants, in whose culture they played a part. Apparently, there still exists a legend blaming a parrot for the multiplicity of tribes. Originally, so the story goes, all people belonged to a single tribe, but two women quarrelled over the ownership of a particular beautiful parrot so the people fell out, each faction blaming its own tribe. Some Indians regarded parrots as holy birds and others believed them to be reincarnated human spirits. Parrots were treated less reverentially by certain groups of native people, who ate them or gave them to their children to play with.

Rainbow lorikeet in flight showing every colour of the spectrum (Donald and Molly Trounson/ Ardea London Ltd)

More Moluccan parrots were discovered as a result of Ferdinand Magellan's ill-fated attempt to find a quick route to the Far East by sailing westwards. Although he was a Portuguese navigator, he sailed under Spanish colours when, in 1519, he headed across the Atlantic. He stopped in Brazil for two weeks, and exchanged a small mirror for ten parrots. He then passed through what we now call the Magellan Straits, and crossed the Pacific to the Philippines where, in 1521, he was tragically killed in a fracas with the natives. A year later, eighteen of his companions made the journey back to Seville, becoming the first people to circumnavigate the globe. Among them was Antonio Pigafetta, an Italian chronicler. His story revealed that they had spent some time in the Moluccas where the parrots took his eye. There were great white parrots called *catara* (cockatoos), and beautifully coloured red ones that were much treasured by the natives for their stunning feathers and exceptionally clear diction. These, the natives called *nori* which eventually gave rise to the name 'lory' that was coined for the fruit-eating species found in that part of South East Asia. The species noted by Pigafetta was probably the chattering lory, a brilliant scarlet bird with green wings and a bright yellow beak.

Not long after the discovery of South America, considerable numbers of parrots were imported into Europe. Even by Tudor times, these birds were an essential part of every courtier's retinue along with his fool and his dogs. As adventurers scoured the world for fresh novelties to delight their royal patrons, an ever greater variety of 'popinjays' – as parrots were called – turned up in courts and menageries. But how many kinds of parrots were known in those days?

During the course of the Renaissance, the medieval Bestiaries were cast aside in favour of more accurately compiled dossiers of God's Creation. These were sometimes written by people who were inspired to get close to the mind of the Almighty by marvelling at His wondrous works. Conrad Gesner, a physician from Zurich, was one such person, and in 1555 produced his *Historia Animalum* in which he described fourteen different kinds of parrot and illustrated them with somewhat heavy and unflattering woodcuts. He faithfully recorded an erroneous observation made a century before by Alvise da Cada Mosto, an Italian who sailed around the west coast of Africa where he

Woodcut of cockatoo from Gesner's Historia Animalum

Woodcut of parrot's nest from Gesner's Historia Animalum *1555*

had seen Senegal parrots. He claimed to have seen parrots building their nests out of twigs and hanging them from branches to protect their eggs and chicks from snakes. Perhaps he had seen the pendulous nests of weaver birds, or even observed lovebirds entering the constructions of social weavers. Gesner produced a picture of a hanging parrot's nest with two snakes foiled in their attempt to raid the contents. It was left to Jean de Lery, a French missionary, to correct the story. While ministering to the souls of the natives in Brazil, he took great pleasure in watching the gaudy parrots which abounded in the countryside and for which the Indians had names. He recorded white-eyed conures, and both orange-winged and mealy amazons. The macaws were called *arat* which ultimately spawned their generic name, *Ara*. The plumage of the blue and yellow macaw he likened to a waistcoat of golden silk and a coat of violet damask. Lery noted its behaviour and recorded that it always placed its nest in a hole in a tree.

Two centuries later, the number of species recorded in zoological inventories had increased to seventy. However, one great group of parrots had yet to enter the European scene; they came from Australia.

AUSTRALIA – REGION OF PARROTS

Although the outstanding navigator, Captain James Cook, is credited with the discovery of Australia in 1770, he and his crew were by no means the first Europeans to set foot ashore and record the strange creatures that lived on that isolated continent. Indeed, Gerard Mercator's map of the world, dated 1569, strongly suggests that the existence of Australia was known to Portuguese mariners well over two centuries before the *Endeavour* put into Botany Bay. This astonishing conclusion arises from the fact that Mercator clearly designated an area in the southern Indian Ocean as Psitacorum Regio (Region of Parrots). The legend states that it is so named because of 'the unheard of size of birds at that place'. It goes on to explain that the sailors who discovered the land were driven there by a powerful wind while heading for Calicut, and followed the coast for 2,000 miles (3,220km) without coming to the end of it. Perhaps they themselves thought they had discovered the great southern continent, Terra Australis,

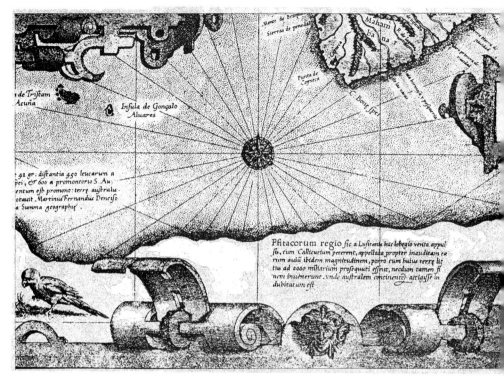

Extract from Gerard Mercator's world map of 1569 carrying the inscription Psitacorum Regio.

whose existence had been postulated in order to 'balance' the world. For some time, however, scholars reckoned that Mercator had acted on fanciful sailors' yarns, because a 10,555km (5,700 nautical mile) crossing of the Indian Ocean was thought to be way beyond the capability of relatively frail Portuguese trading boats. However, recent research by Donald Trounson, a distinguished Australian ornithologist and photographer, has revealed that Mercator's claims may have had some foundation, and that Portuguese mariners were the first Europeans to chance upon Australia and discover some of the unique parrots that live in that part of the world. Circumstantial, but supporting evidence was provided by Dutch traders.

By the end of the sixteenth century, Portugal had fallen as a great marine nation; her fleets had been taken over by her old rival, Spain, and the Dutch had begun to dominate the East Indies trade routes using Portuguese navigation charts. However, in an attempt to try out a faster route to the spice islands, Hendrik Brouwer obtained permission in 1610 to strike out across the Indian Ocean after rounding the Cape of Good Hope, thus taking advantage of the prevailing westerlies rather than beating all the way up the East African coast. The success of the route depended upon prior knowledge of the winds which must have come from the Portuguese pioneers. In due course, all Dutch skippers bound for the Moluccas were instructed to use Brouwer's route. It involved taking an easterly track over the open ocean from the Cape, between latitudes 35 and 44 degrees south for 7,413km (4,000 nautical miles) and then turning north in the Sunda Strait. The problem with this strategy was that the art of precise navigation was still wanting; longitude could not be accurately assessed – sophisticated chronometers were needed for that – and the estimation of distance travelled over the featureless sea was crude in the absence of detailed information about ocean currents. As a consequence, boats taking the Brouwer route faced the danger of overrunning on the easterly leg, and making an unscheduled landfall on the west coast of Australia. This was precisely the fate of one of the first ships to try the course, the *Eendracht*. Captain Dirk Hartog delayed his northward change of course, and on 25 October 1616 came upon Shark Bay in western Australia, or New Holland as it became known.

The *Eendracht* was not the last; over the course of the seventeenth century, at least forty-five Dutch boats came within sight of the Australian coast; some even foundered on it. However, the fact that so many skippers accidentally found themselves 3,150km (1,700 nautical miles) east of their planned turning point suggested that they were unaware of the extra boost given to their boats by the current, the West Wind Drift. The story is worth recounting because it shows that what could happen to Dutch mariners, could equally have happened a century earlier to some of the estimated 620 ships that sailed under the Portuguese flag between Lisbon and the Indies before Spain took the upper hand. A few doubtless made the daunting 10,555km (5,700 nautical mile) crossing of the southern Indian Ocean running before the westerlies and lived to tell the tale about the Region of Parrots. But what were the parrots 'of unheard of size'?

Apart from the macaws, which were not widely known about at the beginning of the sixteenth century, the 'black' cockatoos are the largest parrots in the world. One species, the white-tailed black cockatoo is confined to the southwestern region of the island continent, and is therefore a good candidate for the birds referred to in Mercator's 1569 map. They are magnificent creatures; although reaching 60cm (24in) in length, they have a light buoyant flight, and sometimes assemble in mobs 6,000 strong. They possess conspicuous white under-tail feathers and draw attention to themselves with a loud *kee-ow* call. These super-parrots would certainly have created a lasting impression on weary seamen, glad to be alive after such an arduous and dangerous journey across the open ocean. It may be relevant that the same kind of cockatoo was noted in Captain Nicolas Baudin's log in 1801 when he dropped anchor in Bunker's Cove between Freemantle and Cape Naturaliste. A landing party saw 'birds with large heads and long tails that were white on the underside. They had curved beaks like parrots and made a noise like them'. These were unmistakably white-tailed black cockatoos. Of course, by then, Australia was firmly on the map.

The first substantiated record of an Australian bird refers to a cockatoo which was recorded in July 1606 by Don Diego de Prado y Tovar, who was accompanying Captain Luis Vaez de Torres on an epic journey from South America through the strait that now bears his name. The Spaniards had made landfall in New Guinea, and spent three days at Milne where Prado wrote an account of the avifauna, including the 'numbers of parrots, some very white with a crest of yellow feathers and the beak and feet black'. This is a clear reference to sulphur-crested cockatoos which range across Australia and Papua New Guinea. The description also predates, by a few days, Prado's account of Torres Strait pigeons, plump white birds, which were seen later in the voyage when they sailed westwards blissfully unaware that the land on their port bow was the Great South Land. However, this observation of pigeons flying across the sea is often cited as the first authentic record of an Australian bird. More detailed accounts of Australia's eccentric creatures had to await the arrival of scientific expeditions nearly two centuries later. However, the way was paved by such people as Abel Tasman and William Dampier.

In 1642, Tasman, under Anthony van Dieman, Governor General of the Dutch settlements in the East Indies, discovered Tasmania and, out of deference to his patron, named it Van Dieman's Land. He also circumnavigated Australia. The English buccaneer, Dampier, in his small boat the *Roebuck,* edged into Shark Bay on the west coast of New Holland in August 1699. He was greeted by the sight of cockatoos, and noted that they were 'a sort of white parrot which flew a great many together'. This is a clear reference to little corellas which occasionally gather in huge flocks of 60,000-70,000. Such flocks can make a stand of gum trees seem like a cherry orchard in full bloom. Dampier later returned to England with descriptions of dingoes, curious wallabies and sketches of some of the birds. Although neither Tasman nor Dampier made a profound contribution to our understanding the Australasian region, their sightings and tales did fire the imaginations of people with a more scientific bent. Quite clearly there was a mysterious world waiting to impart its treasures. And all the time, the whereabouts of the great 'missing' continent – Terra Incognita or Terra Australis – tantalised those with a lust for adventure. Cook, the supreme navigator of the eighteenth century, took up the challenge and commanded three scientific expeditions to the South Seas between 1768 and 1779, during which time the discovery of Australian parrots took a great leap forward.

COOK AND THE FIRST FLEET

When HMS *Endeavour* slipped past Plymouth breakwater on 26 August 1768, Cook was under unique and partly secret orders from the Royal Society and the Admiralty. His first objective was to observe the transit of Venus across the face of the sun in Tahiti. But the more clandestine part of his mission was to traverse the southern seas in quest of the Great South Land. It was becoming common practice to include a professional scientific party on such voyages to document fresh wonders of the new world. The person in charge of this side of the operation was Joseph Banks, a newly elected member of the Royal Society with a passion for botany. Under him were people with different enthusiasms and talents including the artist Sydney Parkinson who eventually died of dysentery, but not before he had made more than 1,300 drawings and paintings. Among them was an excellent pencil sketch of a female red-tailed black cockatoo, the oldest known picture of an Australian parrot and now in the British Museum, London.

Having completed his astronomical work in Tahiti, Cook pursued the second half of his mission. He did not sail far enough south to discover Antarctica, but he circumnavigated New Zealand and eventually reached the east coast of New Holland on 19 April 1770. He hauled to in a large sheltered bay that was to become Botany Bay due to the richness of the specimens collected there by Banks and his colleague, Dr Daniel Solander. Here they commented upon the abundance of birds 'of beautiful plumage; among which were two sorts of parroquets and a beautiful loriquet'. Before Cook weighed anchor a Polynesian interpreter, called Tupia, travelling to England procured a rainbow lorikeet which miraculously survived the journey. It was then given to Marmaduke Turnstall in whose possession it was when Peter Brown painted and published a colour engraving of it in his *New Illustrations in Zoology* in 1776. Although a veritable rainbow of colour, he called the bird a blue-bellied parrot. Nevertheless the work of art was the first published picture of an antipodean parrot, and the model for the picture was perhaps the second species of Australian parrot to reach Europe alive, after the sulphur-crested cockatoo. On subsequent expeditions led by Cook to the southern Pacific, George Forster, a German naturalist, was able to depict birds from New Zealand including the kaka; on the same journey he also obtained specimens of the unusual horned parakeet from New Caledonia and a bright red lory from Tahiti. The second proper painting of an Australian parrot was made in 1777 during Cook's last voyage when William Ellis, assistant to the ship's doctor, executed a watercolour of a green rosella killed by William Anderson, the ship's surgeon-naturalist.

When the First Fleet arrived in New South Wales on 20 January 1788 under the command of Captain Arthur Phillip, the crew and passengers were fascinated by the unfamiliar plants and animals which inhabited this antipodean (literally upside-down) world and left them in no doubt that they were entering a land of parrots. Arthur Bowes, a surgeon on board one of the boats, *Lady Penrhyn,* was greatly taken by the bird life on that historic day as they sailed into Port Jackson (now Sydney Harbour), and remarked that 'the singing of various birds among the trees, and the flight of numerous parraquets, lorriquets, cockatoos, and maccaws [sic], made all round seem like enchantment'. Many of those early settlers were inspired to paint what they saw. In several collections dating from the initial settlement there is ample evidence for the prevalence of colourful parrots, including the turquoise parakeet and the quail-like ground parrot. It certainly was a topsy-turvy world where swans were black rather than white, where trees tended to shed their bark rather than their leaves, where mammals hopped and some, like the platypus, laid eggs!

After Cook's explorations and the first settlement, each ship returning home brought its quota of scientific trophies, including living specimens, from the newly discovered parts of the globe. Published journals of the voyages, both official and unofficial, containing descriptions and pictures of exotic creatures and harlequin parrots fuelled the public's imagination, and placed a burden on those who were seriously cataloguing nature. The first person in 'modern' times to attempt to embrace all scientific knowledge in one mammoth encyclopedia was George Louis Leclerc, Compte de Buffon. He came from a distinguished family in Burgundy, and his wealth and social position enabled him to devote his time to biological matters. Between curating the Royal Gardens in Paris, he compiled *Histoire Naturelle,* which appeared in no less than forty-four volumes between 1749 and 1804, the latter ones posthumously. As many as 108 kinds of parrot were known to him, and most of them were illustrated by copperplate engravings. He also documented two instances of successful breeding of captive grey parrots in France, in 1722 and 1774 – a noteworthy record of historical significance. By the time that John Latham started his inventory of birds in 1781, the number of parrots known to science had been significantly enlarged by the discoveries made in the southern seas.

Latham was a medical practitioner, an eminent ornithologist, a fellow of the Royal Society, and probably a friend of Sir Joseph Banks.

His contribution to science was *A General Synopsis of Birds* which attempted to describe all birds known to mankind, including those recorded by Banks and his team. In all, he was able to present 252 'races' of parrots from around the world, including the 'blue-bellied parrot', a 'crested parakeet' in the possession of Banks, and a 'black cockatoo' sketched by Sydney Parkinson but dramatically rendered in colour between the pages of Latham's handbook as the 'Banksian cockatoo'. Then, as now, animals of the same type were sometimes referred to by different vernacular names, leading to a great deal of confusion. A Swedish botanist, Carl Von Linné, solved the problem by assigning scientific names to every kind of animal and plant.

Towards the end of the eighteenth century, many parrots were receiving their proper scientific names based upon Carl Von Linné's binomial system of classification. Basically, he gave every 'species' of creature a position in his catalogue; species which shared certain similarities were then placed into genera, genera were lumped into orders, and orders grouped into classes. Under Linné's arrangement, each kind of animal or plant became registered under a generic and species name, rather like a surname being followed by a Christian name. Thus an African grey parrot became *Psittacus erithacus* the world over. When Linné first drafted his classification in 1735, under the title of *Systema Naturae*, there were relatively few species of parrots for him to name. However, as more specimens turned up in Europe from the tropics, the work had to be frequently revised. In 1788, Johann Gmelin, a German physician and botanist, undertook to edit the thirteenth edition of the book; he incorporated many birds from New Holland and assimilated those in Latham's *Synopsis of Birds*. For the first time, everyone knew that *Psittacus moluccans* referred to the salmon-crested cockatoo, although today it is placed in the genus *Cacatua*. Gmelin also compounded an error made by Latham in the nomenclature he assigned to the green rosella. Latham believed that the specimen portrayed by the brush of Ellis came not from Van Dieman's Land – Tasmania – but from the island of New Caledonia. Gmelin therefore called it *Platycercus caledonicus*, a faulted name by which it is still known today, two centuries later. Such inapppropriate names are not unusual – once registered, many remain for posterity.

During the early part of the nineteenth century, Holland, with her colonial interests in the Far East, was an important centre for the expansion of knowledge about parrots. The prime mover was Konrad Temminck who, in 1820, founded the Rijksmuseum of Natural History in Leiden. From here, he enthused a succession of people to supply specimens from the Dutch East Indies and Australia. It was not without human cost, because several of his collectors succumbed to tropical diseases which they contracted in the tick- and leech-infested forests. Temminck himself gave scientific descriptions of several kinds of parrots including the red-flanked lorikeet, glossy cockatoo, and one sub-species of the sulphur-crested cockatoo. Among those who serviced Temminck was Salomon Müller who spent 11 years in the field, delivering over 500 skins and hundreds of birds eggs. He was especially keen on parrots and discovered several new to science, including one named after him – Müller's parrot. Heinrich Kuhl from Hanover was also fascinated by these birds and wrote a book, *Conspectus Psittacorum*, in 1821 that listed 209 kinds; 18 of them were new, including the slender-billed corella, red-capped parrot and the ultramarine lory from the Marquesas Islands. The next year, Temminck sent him to Java where he secured 2,000 skins to send back to Leiden. 'Hardly a day goes by', he wrote, 'without we discover a new species'. Unfortunately, his days were limited because he died suddenly from a liver infection. The French ornithologist, Louis-Pierre Vieillot, took over where Kuhl left off and went to the West Indies, Australia and the island of Timor.

Several new parrots were named by British zoologists as the nineteenth century wore on. In 1831, Nicholas Vigors, Secretary of the London Zoological Society, was responsible for making the first scientific description of the lovely pink cockatoo from central Australia. He discovered a specimen in the possession of a London taxidermist called Benjamin Leadbeater, and accordingly named it *Cacatua leadbeateri* – Leadbeater's cockatoo. We now know it as Major Mitchell's after the explorer who commented that it greatly enlivened the monotonous colours of the outback! Between 1854 and 1862, several fresh species were discovered by Alfred Russel Wallace during his exploration of the Malay Peninsula and beyond. He was a professional collector and sent back 125,660 specimens to London, including 8,050 birds and the first live birds of paradise to reach Europe. Among the parrots he found were the red-spotted, fairy, and yellow and green lorikeets. He also discovered the Moluccan hanging parakeet, and another species from Flores in the Lesser Sunda Islands is named after him. In 1869 he published a classic account of his journey, *The Malay Archipelago, the Land of the Orang-Utan and the Bird of Paradise,* which he dedicated to Charles Darwin out of 'deep admiration for his genius and his works'. It still makes marvellous reading and includes a fascinating passage on how palm cockatoos manage to crack iron-hard kanary nuts in the Aru Islands.

Wallace's writing inspired a German zoologist, Adolf Meyer, to visit the Celebes and New Guinea area. He discovered a bevy of new lories and lorikeets, and determined that the red and green eclectus parrots were in fact members of the same species, the former being the female and the latter, the male.

By the time Tommaso Salvadori compiled his catalogue of parrots for the British Museum in 1891, he was able to describe 499 different kinds, of which 13 were new species. Admittedly, many of those in Salvadori's book are no longer recognised because he accepted many 'races' or sub-species and gave them full species status. However, the number gives a good idea of the scale of the discoveries that were made during the nineteenth century.

PARROT PORTFOLIOS

Credit for producing the first series of books devoted to the parrot family goes to the French ornithologist, Francois Levaillant. His two-volume set entitled *Histoire Naturelle des Parroquets* dealt with 137 kinds of parrots, and was published between 1801 and 1805. The books were embellished with illustrations by Jacques Barraband, an accomplished draughtsman, which would do justice to any modern work. Such books were important in arousing interest in this group of birds, for artists had a particular role to play in presenting the beauty of parrots to a wide public. After all, through their creative efforts, parrots could be discovered by people who were unable to see these birds in menageries or to visit the parts of the world where they fly free. In the nineteenth century, two English artists did more than anyone else to capture the character and colour of parrots in all their glory – Edward Lear and John Gould.

Lear is perhaps best remembered for his Nonsense Rhymes and ditties. He started life, however, with a promising career as an artist ahead of him; indeed, in many respects, he was a better technician and observer than James Audubon whose reputation was running high when Lear was struggling to establish himself as a serious painter.

Lear was born into a wealthy family in 1812, and largely raised by his sister Ann, twenty-two years his senior. He always took an interest in nature, visiting menageries and poring for hours at a time over Buffon's encyclopedias. Although he had no formal instruction in art,

P

P was a polly
All red blue and green,
The most beautiful polly
That ever was seen.

p !
Poor little Polly!

One of Edward Lear's parrot sketches

he started work as a professional draughtsman at the London Zoo in 1828, and helped to illustrate the society's first guide. But he had greater ambitions. At the time, there was a demand for bird books, lavishly illustrated with coloured engravings or aquatints paid for by subscription, and issued in parts. These would eventually be collated into massive volumes with sumptuous bindings. Audubon had already started his great work, *Birds of America*, in 1827 and printed it on 'double elephant'; the folio included a lovely picture of Carolina parakeets which were still abundant when Audubon secured dead specimens to act as models. Lear decided to capitalize on the prevailing passion for parrots. They were in demand for public and private menageries alike; the Parrot House at the London Zoo was as popular with the visitors as the panda enclosure is today. A cockatoo or macaw was part of the decor of every fashionable literary salon, and a parrot was often a decorative accessory in portraits of aristocratic people; Sir Joshua Reynolds kept one in his studio for this purpose. Furthermore, Meissen and Worcester were both making porcelain parrots, or embellishing some of their products with the images of these handsome, whimsical birds. Lear felt that he could not go wrong.

In November 1830, the first part of his monograph on parrots was published. He called it *Illustrations of the Family of Psittacidae, or Parrots*, and it set a new standard in ornithological illustration. He chose a large-folio format, made his own lithographic engravings and, furthermore, used live birds as his models. As he had not travelled to the tropics to see wild parrots, he sought out birds in the London Zoo or owned by private collectors such as his patron, the Earl of Derby. The results were stunning because he managed to portray the flamboyant birds with a rare sensitivity combined with an exacting scientific realism; the detail was so exceptionally good that feathers appeared to lift from the surface of the pages. What was more, the parrots were 'alive'; Lear had caught them swaying on their perches, or preening, or just looking mischievous in the way that only parrots can. His birds were very much portraits of particular individuals rather than stylized representations of their species. But although the work was a triumph of artistic achievement for a young lad of twenty, it fell short of Lear's financial expectations. He had hoped to issue the monograph in 14 parts, it clearly says so on the cover of the first one. He only managed 12 over the course of the next 2 years, depicting 42 kinds of parrots. In all, 175 sets were produced, many of which Lear probably gave away. Over the years, some of the plates have endured as popular prints, especially his macaws. The original sets of lithographs are worth a fortune. One of his *Illustrations of the Family of Psittacidae, or Parrots* was sold at auction in New York in 1989 for $231,000 (£147,000).

With the passing of the years, Lear became dogged by ill-health and fading eyesight. In the absence of proper recognition for his talents by his contemporaries, his enthusiasm for wildlife art waned. However, for a short period he did undertake engraving work for John Gould who, sadly, erased his name from the plates. By contrast, Gould was an immediate success. A self-taught naturalist, he developed into an entrepreneur responsible for publishing a massive sumptuous collection of lithographs of wildlife from Australia and New Guinea. They are greatly valued even today; his portrait of a pair of Major Mitchell's cockatoos with the crest erected in a blaze of colour fetches upwards of £10,000, thus rating as one of the most valuable parrot pictures in the world, second only to an original of Audubon's Carolina parakeets.

Born in 1801, the son of a Dorset gardener, John Gould became a good botanist, an excellent taxidermist, and liked to be known as 'The Bird Man'. The Zoological Society of London employed him in 1827 for his talents at stuffing animals; this is where he became acquainted with Edward Lear. Gradually, he developed a fascination for the creatures of New Holland, Australia. Although he was a capable draughtsman, his wife Elizabeth had a far greater talent, indeed she was a first-rank artist. She also had two brothers who had settled in the Hunter Valley of New South Wales. The letters and specimens they sent back to London fired Gould's interest in Australia all the more. This became manifest in 1837 when he produced a four-part synopsis, *The Birds of Australia and Adjacent Islands*, illustrated by Elizabeth. Gould was disappointed with the work, so in 1838 he packed his bags and travelled to Australia accompanied by his family and John Gilbert, a professional zoological collector. On arrival at their destination, the two men made a series of expeditions into the bush, collecting specimens, making field notes and sketching everything that moved, while Elizabeth worked furiously making 600 or more drawings of birds and mammals. She also applied herself to the task of committing the images of trees and their foliage, and general scenics, to paper, and these would ultimately be used as delicate backgrounds to enhance the portraits in Gould's major works. After eighteen months, the family returned to England, leaving Gilbert to maintain a steady supply of skins. Sadly, Elizabeth died shortly afterwards in childbirth aged only thirty-seven.

Gould the impresario, pressed on and employed a team of fine artists including Lear to present his subjects in the best possible light, and produce thousands of hand-coloured lithographed prints for his magnificent part work, *The Birds of Australia*. Each consisted of 600 plates, 54 of which were parrots. He illustrated all the species known to him, from the smallest to the characterful cockatoos. His birds were depicted, like Lear's, in great detail and in vivid colour, and were full of life. Between 1840 and 1848, 250 sets were produced in 36 parts at a price of £115 per set; today a single plate would fetch several times this amount. However, there was no shortage of subscribers; among Gould's customers were 107 libraries, 12 monarchs, 16 dukes, 30 earls, 5 counts, 61 baronets and one bishop. Gould had spent £15,000 on the enterprise, but was well recompensed for his project which stands today as a marvellous 'window' on colonial natural history. Two decades later, he brought out a supplement which included plates of the lovely golden-shouldered and princess (Alexandra's) parakeets and the larger New Zealand species. In 1875, he issued another set of outstanding plates in *The Birds of New Guinea and the Adjacent Papuan Islands;* it included the birds of paradise in all their extrovert finery and a further 47 pictures of parrots, which gleam from the pages like jewels.

John Gould also performed a service to those who liked to have the company of exotic birds in or around their own homes. When he returned from Australia in 1840, he brought with him some small, living parakeets that were destined to become the universally popular cage bird, known by a corruption of their aboriginal name as 'the budgerigar'. Their dinky appearance, glowing green coloration, and ability to mimic made them a sensational success.

Sadly, the meeting between men and parrots was not always marked by joyous, scientific revelation. Indeed, for some birds, as we shall see in the next chapter, the encounter with Europeans was fatal.

Mascarene Parrots

5 · PARROTS PAST

Over the past three centuries, at least ten kinds of parrots have gone the same way as the dodo, and today many others are in danger of following it into the pages of history books. Species are not immortal. Indeed, for most, extinction is a natural outcome of the evolutionary process. After all, change is brought about partly by success and failure between different kinds of creatures competing for resources needed for their survival. The winners establish themselves and, by implication, the less able ones die out. As a consequence, a veritable pageant of species has passed across the world's stage, some staying longer than others. All of them ultimately make an exit, nudged off by actors better able to perform in the play of life. Today, the problem is caused by the high rate at which animals and plants are vanishing from the scene, and we are solely responsible.

Birds are faced with an extra difficulty, because they may be generally on the decline. According to the fossil record, birds may have reached a peak of diversity 250,000 years ago, when there were perhaps 11,500 species. Many may have perished in the repeated glaciations during the Ice Ages, which resulted in the 9,000 or so species living today. However, the losses are continuing at an accelerated pace due to the impact of people on places where birds live. One of the keys to our own success has been our talent for altering the land to suit our needs and, in doing so, destroying it for many wild creatures that enjoyed it before our arrival. Accordingly, human progress has been punctuated by the frequent loss of wild species.

Of the parrots that have become extinct in historical times, the best documented is the Carolina parakeet which, having coexisted with the native people of North America, proved to be suicidally sensitive to the spread of European civilization.

THE LAST NORTH AMERICAN PARAKEETS

Some time during the late 1880s, a consignment of sixteen pretty, green and yellow parakeets was delivered to the zoo in Cincinnati, Ohio. They were not expensive, each one costing a mere $2.50. Three decades later, however, the value of the pair that survived soared to an astonishing $4,000. Even at this inflated price, the zoo managers were not tempted to cash in their profit because, by then, the little birds were literally irreplaceable – they were the last Carolina parakeets in captivity, and possibly the last of their kind on earth. The couple of Carolina parakeets owned by Cincinnati Zoo were christened Lady Jane and Incas; they had languished in a cage for thirty-two years, and had been way beyond their prime for breeding since the turn of the twentieth century. Indeed, birds of this species had never shown a proclivity for successful nesting in aviaries, and so zoos were utterly dependent upon a supply of wild caught birds for replenishing their stocks. Now that the sources had dried up, the zoo had no way of replacing the pair of ageing parakeets.

The doomed couple were in distinguished company at Cincinnati because in a neighbouring cage was Martha, a passenger pigeon. She was the only surviving representative of this intensely social species that was once so abundant in swathes of North American countryside that migrating flocks 'darkened the sky' and 'the weight of the numbers broke great branches from trees'. Sadly, Martha was to die alone, when she was about twenty-nine years old. Her keeper discovered her

CINCINNATI TIMES-STAR

FRIDAY, FEBRUARY 22, 1918

FAR-FAMED LAST PARRAKEET OF ITS KIND IS MOURNED AT ZOO

Sol. Stephan, Superintendent of the Garden, Believes That Grief Was a Contributing Cause — Will Have the Body Stuffed.

A student of bird-life, acting as coroner in the case of "Incas," the Carolina parrakeet, said to be the last of its race, might enter a verdict of "died of old age." But General Manager Sol. A. Stephan of the Zoo, whose study of birds goes farther than mere physical structure, development and decay knows the bird died of grief. "Incas," coveted by many zoological gardens, died Thursday night surrounded by his genuinely sorrowing friends, Col. Stephan and the keepers. Late last summer, "Lady Jane," the mate of Incas for 32 years, passed away, and after that the ancient survivor was a listless and mournful figure, indeed. In recent years Col. Stephan received many large offers for Incas and Lady Jane and the New York Zoo was especially eager to obtain the birds. After the death of the female, various zoos renewed offers for the survivor, but Col. Stephan would not part with the bird. Just how old the parrakeet was is not known. The bird was well-aged when it, with its mate, was obtained by the Zoo 32 years ago.

"The Carolina parrakeet family was the only real American parrot," said Colonel Stephan, Friday. "There was a time when the family was a numerous one. But a curious trait in the make-up of the family proved its undoing. The parrakeets would fly in thick flocks and, if a hunter fired into them, they would wheel and come right back to the scene of the shooting as if curious to see what caused the explosion and to learn why some of their number fell to the ground. So by their foolishness the Carolina parrakeets gradually were shot out of existence as a family."

Colonel Stephan will have the bird mounted and, in accordance with a promise made by him some years ago, will present the specimen to the Smithsonian Institution.

Announcement in the Cincinnati Times-Star of the death of the last Carolina parakeet lifeless body on the floor of her cage at 13.00 hours on 1 September 1914. At that moment, the passenger pigeon became officially extinct. However, the geriatric parakeets lingered a few years longer. Lady Jane expired during late summer of 1917, after which her mate, Incas, became listless as though mourning for his departed companion. He eventually died on the evening of 21 February 1918, apparently surrounded by his genuinely sorrowful friends.

To mark the tragic passing of this, yet another, species in the same zoo, the *Cincinnati Times-Star* ran an obituary the following day with the headline, 'Far-famed Last Parrakeet [sic] of its Kind is Mourned at Zoo.' Colonel Stephan, the zoo's superintendent, acted as coroner and came to the conclusion that, although old age was a contributory factor, 'grief' was the chief cause of death. The pathetic little corpse was allegedly packaged and sent to the Smithsonian Museum for 'stuffing', and to be placed alongside the historic remains of Martha, but it apparently never arrived. From the scientific point of view, the disappearance of Incas was no great loss because over 700 Carolina parakeet skins and mounted specimens are preserved in museum collections around the world. Luckily, there are sufficient contemporary accounts to piece together a fairly comprehensive picture of these parakeets in their heyday, and the story of their decline.

The first European settlers in North America to encounter Carolina parakeets by the hundred would have never predicted such an ignominious end because these birds were once widespread east of the Great Plains, occurring in flocks of up to 300. On the basis of size and colour, the species was divided into two races; the typical form lived in the eastern states, whereas the larger and slightly duller birds were found west of the Appalachian Mountains, where they were often referred to as Louisiana parakeets. For parrots, they were hardy birds and able to cope with the vicissitudes of the North American climate; the flocks were not migratory and so, in winter, the birds were often seen flying over the countryside when snow lay thickly on the ground. Some accounts indicate that frigid weather caused the birds to go torpid, and so prevented them emerging from their roosting holes. This observation has, however, been disputed.

Carolina parakeets preferred heavily forested river valleys with large trees festooned with mosses and lichens. These provided the birds with plenty of hollows for roosting and nesting. Early in the morning, the birds left their roosts and ranged widely in fast flying flocks to feed on the seeds of maples, elms, cypresses and pines. But their favourite food seemed to be the tough-shelled seeds of cocklebur, a common plant that became a serious weed to the farmers pushing westwards across the continent. James Audubon recorded the habits of the birds as they arrived at their feeding area. They were wary, and did not settle at once, tending to circle at a considerable height, 'gradually lowering until they almost touch the ground, when suddenly re-ascending, they all settle on the tree that bears the fruit'. Like all parrots, they used their bills to assist them to climb, indeed they had no regard for whether they were right side up or not. Certainly they seemed more at home in the branches than on the ground, where they were apparently so slow and awkward that people could sometimes walk up to them. Around the middle of the day, the screeching parakeets took a siesta, first flying to drinking spots and then retiring to the tops of trees where they whiled away the time, grooming and resting. The quest for food was resumed towards the end of the afternoon and continued until dusk, whereupon the noisy, chattering flocks sped back to the roosts. These were usually hollow stumps wherein each individual suspended itself from the wall by its beak and feet.

Unfortunately, their reproductive arrangements are not very well documented. The parakeets probably nested in loose colonies. Both Audubon and the North American ornithologist, Alexander Wilson, stated that the birds nested in groups and laid their eggs at the bottom of cavities, indicating that several hens may have contributed to the clutch. Cooperative breeding of this kind is very unlikely for a parrot. Other secondhand accounts which are equally incredible refer to these small parakeets building flimsy nests at the ends of branches. What is certain is that the birds nested in holes, laid white eggs, perhaps 2-3 in a clutch, and that both parents fed the chicks.

Sadly, no amount of breeding of captive birds could prevent the implacable decline in the Carolina parakeet population caused by the systematic colonization of the North American continent by Europeans. As more and more land was settled, the range occupied by the birds became steadily smaller until, by the middle of the nineteenth century, the birds were restricted to the swamps of Florida and the Mississippi Basin. Several factors contributed to the parakeet's demise. Clearance of the forests to make way for agriculture obviously deprived the parrots of their favourite habitat. It has even been suggested that the introduction of honey bees from Europe posed a subtle threat; the bees escaped into the wildwoods ahead of the settlers and possibly took over hollow trees that would otherwise have been occupied by families of parakeets. Without a doubt, the settlers themselves never lost an opportunity to demolish trees occupied by bees to steal their honey, and such a practice would have taken many good nest sites out of commission. Huge numbers of the birds were netted for the pet trade, although Audubon did not rate them very highly: 'their screams are so disagreeable as to render them at best very indifferent companions'. He did, however, suggest a rather unusual method for coercing the birds into being wonderfully 'tame – by frequently dunking them in water. Is it to be wondered that the parakeets had little talent for mimicking the human voice? But if they were found to be wanting as pets, the birds had other uses. They made good eating. Many a parakeet that invited itself to feed on cultivated land ended up braised or stewed on the farmer's table. Many were also killed and divested of their pretty green feathers for the glorification of women's headgear. Later in the century (1886) a poll was conducted of hats being worn in the streets of New York; 542 out of 700 incorporated fully mounted birds as part of the decor.

However, it was the Carolina parakeet's appetite for crops that led to its ruin. Had these attractive and unique parrots kept to their traditional diet of native tree-seeds and cockleburs, they might conceivably have been around today. Unfortunately, some of the produce grown by the people who were taming the wilderness was very much to the parakeets' taste. Where once flocks of gluttonous little parrots had crawled over the stems of native weeds, they now turned their attention to the nutritious fare planted by the settlers. Foraging in flocks, the birds could devastate a crop in a very short space of time, which made them heartily hated by the farmers.

Carolina Parrot Males 1, 2, 3 Females 4, 5

PSITTACUS CAROLINENSIS,

Plant Vulgo. Cuckle Burr

Drawn & Published by John J. Audubon F.R.S.U. M.W.S.   Engraved, Printed & Colored by R. Havell, London.

Parrots Past

In 1831, Audubon gave a comprehensive account of the conflict between parrots and people. He wrote:

> The stacks of grain put up in a field are resorted to by flocks of these birds, which frequently cover them so entirely, that they present to the eye the same effect as if a brilliantly coloured carpet had been thrown over them. They cling around the whole stack, pull out straws, and destroy twice as much grain as would suffice to satisfy their hunger. They assail Pear and Apple-trees, where the fruit is yet very small and far from ripe, and this merely for the sake of the seeds . . . and as if through sheer mischief, pluck off the fruits, open them up to the core, and, if disappointed at the sight of the seeds, which are yet soft and of a milky consistence, drop the apple or pear, and pluck another, passing from branch to branch, until the trees which were before so promising, are left completely stripped.

Almost every kind of fruit planted was grist to the sharp bills of the parakeets – mulberries, pecan nuts and grapes were devastated if the birds were given a free rein; in Florida, the 'sunshine state', the predatory parrots cut off young green oranges and peaches before the fruit had a chance to form.

Audubon described the increasingly dim view that the hard-pressed landowners took of the toll exacted on their crops. 'Do not imagine', he wrote 'that all these outrages are borne without severe retaliation on the part of the planters.' The flocks of feeding parakeets were quite approachable, and the farmers shot them relentlessly. However, the scale of the slaughter was enhanced by the peculiar behaviour of the birds themselves under fire. After the first discharge, instead of swiftly winging away out of danger, the flocks tended to return and wheel around, screeching over their dead and dying companions, even landing once again on the stack of grain or stand of trees on which they were originally feeding. Under natural circumstances, such apparently heroic behaviour might be of advantage to the survivors. For instance, by gathering around a companion stricken down by a

Carolina parakeets from James Audubon's Birds of America *Vol I (by courtesy of the Natural History Museum)*

Carolina Parakeets lingering around a dying companion

hawk or falcon, the predator might be deterred by the mobbing birds
from launching another attack because it had lost the element of surprise. Such behaviour, designed to minimise the lethal effects of
natural enemies, helped the farmers to conserve their fruit but did
little to preserve the Carolina parakeets in the face of fire-arms. Every
shot brought down ten or more parakeets until there were so few left
that it was not worth discharging more powder. Audubon witnessed
the suicidal behaviour, and saw hundreds destroyed in the course of a
few hours on one farm, procuring a basketful in order to select specimens as models for his splendid aquatint.

The population of Carolina parakeets could not sustain such a
slaughter indefinitely. Even during Audubon's lifetime, the birds had
been disappearing from west of the Mississippi, and from the eastern
part of its range. By the second half of the nineteenth century, the
flocks of chattering little parrots were confined to two locations, one
in Florida and the other in Oklahoma.

As the century drew to a close, the wanton destruction of birds for sport, feathers and aviculture was elevated to the status of a national pastime. The birds were being consumed so fast that spokesmen in their defence began to band together and conscript others to the cause of protection. Words bristling with emotion were penned by Dr William Hornaday, director of the New York Zoological Park. He wrote:

> The thing that stares me in the face every waking hour, like a grisly spectre with bloody fang and claw, is *the extermination of species.* To me, that is a horrible thing. It is whole-sale murder, no less. It is a capital crime, and a black disgrace to the races of civilized mankind.

Unfortunately, such sentiments and the legislation championed by protectionists to safeguard beleaguered wildlife were too late for the passenger pigeon, Hudsonian godwit, Eskimo curlew and North America's unique parakeet. Three distinguished ornithologists, Spencer Baird, Dr Thomas Brewer and Dr Robert Ridgeway, warned of the parrot's impending doom in their book *The Birds of North America* published in 1874. 'There is little doubt that their total extermination is only a matter of years, perhaps to be consummated within the lifetime of persons now living.' They were not far out.

The last authentic wild Carolina parakeet was collected on Paget Creek, Brevard Country, Florida by Dr E. A. Mearns on 18 April 1901. There was a further reliable sighting in April 1904 of two flocks totalling thirteen birds at Taylor's Creek, on the north-east side of Lake Okeechobee. However, even after the death of Lady Jane and Incas, ornithologists nurtured the hope that a few parakeets survived deep in some remote swamp forest. During spring of 1926, that wish appeared to come true when Charles E. Doe, curator of birds at the University of Florida, saw three pairs of green and yellow parakeets on a hummock in Kissimmee Prairie, Okeechobee County, Florida. He confidently identified them as Carolina parakeets, and even took five eggs which are still in the possession of the museum in Gainsville. Unfortunately, they could have been laid by any number of small parrots and so they are useless as corroborating evidence. With so many exotic birds flying around the Florida countryside, Doe's sighting has never been unquestionably accepted. Neither has an observation made a decade later along the Santee River, South Carolina.

Unlike most records of species thought to be long since extinct, this one was made by experienced and reliable bird watchers. The location was 4,850 ha (12,000 acres) of heavily timbered swamp leased in 1934 to George Malamphy for observing turkeys. While crouching in his hides, he discovered more than turkeys – or so he claimed. Within a year, he had seen ivory-billed woodpeckers on thirty-three occasions, sometimes three birds together. Then as now, this, the largest and most flamboyant of American woodpeckers, was on the brink of extinction, and so Malamphy's records were of exceptional interest. He related his sightings to Alexander Sprunt, supervisor of the National Audubon Society's southern sanctuaries based in Charleston, and to Herbert Stoddard of Thomasville, Georgia. They were impressed by Malamphy's knowledge and decided to go up the Santee River to see for themselves. However, as if rare ivory-bills were not sufficient, Malamphy nonchalantly announced that he had seen something even more sensational – Carolina parakeets! On eight or nine occasions, little green parrots had put in an appearance in front of his turkey 'blinds'. Once, no less than seven flew down to devour the sunflower seeds put out to lure the big game-birds to within range of his hide.

On their first visit, neither Sprunt nor Stoddard saw signs of the parakeets. But late in 1936 they returned with Robert Porter Allen, director of sanctuaries for the National Audubon Society, to survey the swamps in an all-out effort to locate the last Carolina parakeets. They established baited feeding stations to bring the birds out of hiding. On 28 November their preparations were apparently rewarded when Sprunt reported seeing a single 'dove-like bird, definitely green in the bright sunlight'. It shot over his head and disappeared rapidly towards the swamp. Five days later, on a rather dark winter afternoon, Sprunt spotted two likely parakeets and, when Allen joined him, three birds hurtled past them. Similar sightings were made until 11 December. After considering the possibility that they had mistakenly identified mourning doves and escaped foreign parakeets, they pronounced these birds Carolina parakeets. Despite much searching, none were seen the following year. But in 1938, another observer reported being mobbed by two green parakeets with yellow heads; on investigation, a 'young bird' fluttered from nearby bushes. No other plausible sightings were made. Today, the area is developed and useless as a sanctuary for either ivory-bills or parakeets.

Perhaps a vestigial population of Carolina parakeets did linger on in the Santee Swamp for twenty or so years after Incas finally fell from his perch in Cincinnati Zoo. However, with the passage of time even Robert Allen, who accompanied Sprunt, became sceptical. Although he felt that the parakeets were present, the birds seen in poor light at dusk on several occasions could well have been doves. Maybe the others were the result of wishful thinking. We will never know.

THE PATTERN OF PARROT EXTINCTION

The Carolina parakeet was the most recent member of the family to become history. The fact that it was the only species confined to North America made its disappearance particularly regrettable. None has yet been lost from the mainland of Africa, South East Asia, or South America, although the little blue or Spix's and Lear's macaws from Brazil are becoming perilously close to extinction and have probably vanished from the wild. On the other hand, parrots confined to islands, especially those in the Caribbean and Indian Ocean, have proved very vulnerable when their havens have been invaded and colonized. Like so many creatures that have evolved in isolation, sometimes in the absence of mammalian predators, their relatively small populations are composed of individuals that are often tame and confiding, and which easily succumb to human hunters or their camp followers like rats and cats.

Scholars of parrot extinction run into problems when trying to assess exactly how many species have been annihilated since the great Age of Discovery. With a few kinds, the evidence can be handled. Seven extinct parrots, including the Carolina parakeet, are known from their skins preserved in museum collections. There is therefore no doubt about the validity of the Society and black-fronted parakeets from Raiatea and Tahiti respectively; Newton's parakeet and the

Mascarene parrot certainly used to live on the Mascarene Islands in the Indian Ocean, and Cuba once boasted its own red macaw. The paradise parakeet from Australia was well observed until fifty years ago, and there are photographs of the bird as well. A further two species are widely accepted on the basis of bones and good descriptions by early travellers. On Mauritius lived the broad-billed parrot, and another rather similar species occurred on Rodriguez. However, there are many 'hypothetical' parrots which exist only as sketches or descriptions in notebooks, and have never been examined properly in the flesh by competent naturalists, or collected and placed in museums. Walter Rothschild was faced with this problem when he published his sumptuous and hefty book, *Extinct Birds*, in 1907. He listed another 3 kinds of parrots and 5 species of Caribbean macaw, none of which is recognised today. The difficulty often stems from the nature of the original descriptions, and the fact that parrots were indiscriminately transported by humans from place to place. If a seventeenth-century explorer claimed to have seen blue and yellow macaws flying in the forests of a West Indian island, there is no way of telling today if the birds were genuine natives belonging to an indigenous species, or whether they were of imported stock belonging to the familiar South American species. Even so, Guadaloupe may have had its own amazon parrot and a unique conure, but in the absence of incontrovertible evidence they remain 'hypothetical' parrots.

DEATH IN THE MASCARENES

Between 645 and 805 km (400 and 500 miles) east of Madagascar, lie three islands of volcanic origin – Mauritius, Rodriguez and Reunion. Surrounded by the tepid blue waters of the Indian Ocean, they were once tropical paradises. The grand mountains from which crystal-clear streams flowed were covered with lush forests, and these were

The deadly trade in wild parrots; Senegal parrots crammed into a cage ready for shipment (Dave Curry/EIA)

Parrot appeal – a pair of peach-faced lovebirds sitting in contact; they breed well in captivity (Jean-Michel Labat/Ardea London Ltd)

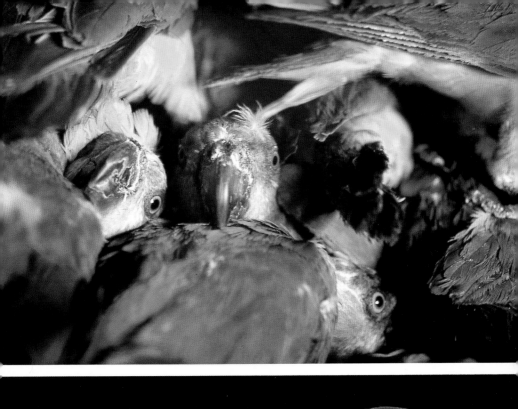

populated chiefly by absurdly tame birds and reptiles which had evolved in splendid isolation and with nothing to fear. Among them was a bevy of parrots unique to the islands and, perhaps weirdest of all birds, the dodos and solitaires. For perhaps millions of years they had enjoyed a fool's paradise because none was equipped for coping with the drastic changes made by human settlers. Of 28 kinds of birds endemic to the islands, 25 failed to survive for long after the first seafarers put ashore.

The islands were certainly known to the Portuguese, indeed they are named after one of their navigators, Mascarenhas, who came upon them in 1505. However, the first to give an account of one of the islands and of its unusual inhabitants was a Dutch explorer. In 1598, Admiral Jacob van Neck landed on Mauritius, the second largest of the Mascarenes, and he and his men discovered numbers of gross, flightless birds the size of turkeys, which they referred to as *dod-aarsen* (dodos). To them, the confiding dodos must have seemed like manna from heaven. After all, the sailors were driven by the conviction that all creatures were placed on earth by God for the benefit of man. Islands richly endowed with edible birds could only be regarded by scurvy-ridden mariners as chandlers' stores for provisioning their ship's galley. Despite the fact that dodo flesh could scarcely be rendered tender even by prolonged boiling, many birds were taken aboard and eaten. However, they were not the only creatures used for victualling the boat. A contemporary print used to illustrate van Neck's journal shows his crew 'revelling in the abundance of this virgin isle' by catching and clubbing parrots to death. These probably belonged to the species referred to in his chronicle as 'the many grey parrots'. Wolphart Harmanszoon, who subsequently visited Mauritius between 1601 and 1602, made a drawing which shows a rather heavy parrot with a relatively massive bill and a jaunty crest surmounting its forehead. Harmanszoon's manuscript, drawing and all, is in the library of the Rijksuniversiteit in Utrecht. Later, Sir Thomas Herbert,

Flock of Australian galahs (Jean-Paul Ferrero/Ardea London Ltd)

Little corellas at a farmyard in Cloncurry, Queensland, Australia (Jean-Paul Ferrero/Ardea London Ltd)

Admiral van Neck's crew catching parrots for the pot on Mauritius in 1598

an English traveller, thought he saw cockatoos when he landed on the island in 1627. It was as yet unsettled, but he recorded the fact that the parrots were 'very numerous', although apparently untamable. He included a woodcut of the 'cacato' in his book *A Relation of some Yeares Travaile, begunne Anno 1626* published in 1634.

The parrot seen by these first visitors to Mauritius belonged to a unique species. It was comparatively large, being about 70cm (28in) long, and is known today as the broad-billed parrot (*Lophopsittacus mauritianus*). As its common name states, the beak was very wide; but it was lightly constructed and possibly designed for scooping fruit pulp rather than for cracking tough seeds. The wings were probably stubby; like so many terrestrial birds confined to islands, the power of flight may have slightly deteriorated. There is also evidence to suggest that the degree of sexual dimorphism may have been very marked. Little else is known about this large and aberrant parrot because within a few years none was left alive on Mauritius. Some were seen in about 1638, but by the time a German preacher, Johann Hoffman, arrived

142

Woodcut of 'a cacato' from Sir Thomas Herbert's A relation of some Yeares
Travaile, begunne Anno 1626

on the island in 1673 for a two-year stay, he was unable to find any grey parrots. By then, the place had become settled, the forest cut back, and a host of creatures let loose to compete with or predate upon the native wildlife. Pigs and goats were introduced as early as 1602, to establish a stock that could be later cropped for food by the crews of passing ships. The pigs alone were capable of devastating the ground nests of tortoises and dodos. Rats and monkeys followed. For trusting parrots which need over-mature, hollow trees for nesting, the new wave of invaders, including musket-wielding men, proved to be disastrous, and around the middle of the seventeenth century the broad-billed parrot became extinct. In doing so, it had the dubious distinction of being the first casualty of human contact with the Mascarene Islands. Others were to follow, the best known being the dodo. A few were probably still alive in 1681, but there was no mention of them a decade later when a full inventory was made of the birds of Mauritius.

Parrots fared no better on the larger neighbouring island of Reunion, then called Bourbon. In 1618, Willem Bontekoe van Hoorn left the Dutch island of Texel bound for India via the Cape of Good Hope. Unfortunately, he did not reach his destination as expected because his ship caught fire and exploded, though luckily he survived by clinging to a piece of floating wreckage which was spotted by a passing boat. The one object that he managed to save was his log which enabled him in 1646 to publish an account of his adventures. Apparently, he and his crew spent three weeks on Reunion where they discovered 'many geese, pigeons, parrots and other birds which could be killed in crowds'. His narrative continues:

> The most amazing thing is that when we catch a parrot or other bird and pinch it a bit so that it shrieks, all the others that were in the neighbourhood come by as if they wanted to free it, and were therefore taken. We went back to the ship with a load of feathered food.

Like Mauritius, Reunion was used from the very beginning as a place to victual ships, and so the omens were not favourable for the survival of another unique species of parrot.

The Mascarene parrot – (*Mascarinus mascarinus*) as it became known – was a very distinguished bird and an unusually coloured one. An excellent description was given by Pére du Bois who visited Reunion between 1669 and 1672. He saw parrots a little larger than pigeons, light grey in general coloration but with black face-masks and large beaks 'the colour of fire'. Alas, the birds were doomed. Following settlement, there was widescale deforestation to make way for the inevitable plantations of sugar cane, banana, vanilla and coffee trees. With such drastic alterations to the island's vegetation, the fate of the parrots was sealed, and by the early part of the nineteenth century the Mascarene parrot had vanished from Reunion. Luckily, live ones were brought to Europe, giving zoologists a chance to take a good look at them. The last living Mascarene parrot may have been owned by King Maximilian of Bavaria, who kept it in his zoological gardens where its portrait was painted for C. W. Hahns's *Ornithologischer Atlas* published between 1834 and 1841. Otherwise all that remains of this singular parrot are a few skins preserved in museums.

Rodriguez was also severely abused by the European colonists. Lying nearly 645km (400 miles) east of Mauritius, it is the smallest of the Mascarenes and was once completely covered by forest. Only nine kinds of terrestrial and freshwater birds are known to have lived on the island, including at least one parrot. The first settlers arrived in 1691. They were religious refugees, Huguenots from France, led by François Leguat. They stayed two years then left, so it is said, to seek women on Mauritius; but were jailed instead by the Dutch Governor. Afterwards Leguat returned to France and, in 1708, gave an account of his adventures. Among the birds he described and sketched on Rodriguez was the solitaire, a relative of the dodo which may have survived until about 1791. He also saw many small parrots which today are called Newton's parakeet (*Psittacula excul*). They caught plenty for the pot – the birds apparently made good eating – and made pets of others which they taught to speak. Leguat took one able to speak Flemish and French on their ill-fated trip to Mauritius.

Newton's parakeet belonged to a group of Afro-Asian ringed parakeets of the genus *Psittacula*, which have invaded several islands in the Indian Ocean including the Seychelles where the birds evolved

Society Parakeet

Black-fronted Parakeet

Newton's Parakeet

Mascarene Parrot

Paradise Parakeet

Cuban Macaw

In the shadow
of the Dodo

into separate species. Those on Rodriguez were quite distinctive. Most ringed parakeets are green in colour with black collars, but those recorded by Leguat were basically blue. Sadly, only two specimens were collected and sent to England for examination by bird taxonomists. One was received by Professor Alfred Newton, eminent founder member of the British Ornithologist's Union and author of *The Dictionary of Birds* (1896), after whom the species is named. Both skins are in Cambridge University museum, the sole remnants of this striking parrot because no living ones were seen after about 1870.

A similar fate befell the related Seychelles parakeet (*Psittacula wardi*), which died out at approximately the same time. The birds developed a taste for maize planted by the settlers, so they were ruthlessly shot and trapped. Forest clearance to make space for coconut palms may also have nudged the birds towards extinction.

Rodriguez may have been inhabited by yet another kind of parrot. Bones, including a complete skull, found on the island indicate the existence of a super-parrot with an outsize bill, resembling the broad-billed species from Mauritius to which it was probably related. Contemporary accounts appear to confirm its presence. The anonymous author of a manuscript written around 1730, known as *Relation de l'Ile Rodriguez*, was one of the first visitors to the place to write down what he saw. He describes a long-tailed parrot, bigger than a pigeon, with large head and bill and green in colour. He recorded that most of the birds lived on islets to the south of Rodriguez, where they consumed little black seeds from a tree the leaves of which had the aroma of lemon. The parrots flew to the main island to drink, presumably because there was no fresh water on the coral cays where they were feeding. These cockatoo-sized birds, now called the Rodriquez parrot (*Necropsittacus rodericanus*), may still have been in evidence when, in 1761, the island was visited by a French astronomer, Alexandre Guy Pingre, to observe the planet Venus. He clearly noted two kinds of parrots which he called *perroquet* and *perruche*, the former referring to Newton's parakeets, the latter to the larger Rodriguez parrot. Unfortunately, this heavy beaked species became extinct sometime during the eighteenth century before anyone bothered to collect skins or to record the details of how they lived.

The Mascarene Islands have been severely despoiled since they were discovered, and what remain of the indigenous species are still suffering from loss of native forest and also from predation or competition by introduced mammals and birds. Today, eleven kinds of endangered birds, like the Mauritius kestrel and pink pigeon, survive albeit precariously. The Mauritius parakeet, which rivals the kestrel for the status of being one of the rarest birds in the world, was once numerous but is now reduced to a population of less than a dozen birds. Unless the current breeding programme proves to be a success, this species will follow the related Newton's parakeet into extinction.

MYSTERY OF THE MISSING MACAWS

The first European mariners to visit the West Indies were possibly led to land by flights of parrots (see Chapter 4). Once ashore, they were certainly impressed by the exotic birds. However, it is sometimes difficult to assess what they saw because their descriptions may have referred to birds brought as pets to the islands from South America by the native people, and subsequently let loose. This is especially true of the macaws which were observed on the Caribbean islands, many of which used to be assigned specific status on the basis of historical accounts.

The West Indies run for over 2,000km (1,240 miles) between the Florida peninsula and the coast of Venezuela. They are divided into three groups. To the north, the Bahamas are low, dry islands made of coral limestone. The central group, or Greater Antilles, embraces the large mountainous islands of Cuba, Jamaica, Hispaniola and Puerto Rico. The Lesser Antilles form a barrier between the Atlantic Ocean and the Caribbean Sea, and are smaller although some, like Guadeloupe and Grenada, rise to nearly 1,000m (3,280ft) above sea level. Their tropical climates are all tempered by the trade winds and they are frequently lashed by destructive cyclones. Such storms have undoubtedly assisted land-based birds from neighbouring continents to colonize the islands. This is probably how the amazons, conures and macaws reached the West Indies. Furthermore, once 'marooned', the populations tended to evolve independently from each other, thus leading to the development of species unique to individual islands. The amazon parrots are a case in point. In the Lesser Antilles, there are no less than four species; St Lucia, St Vincent, and Dominica possess their own quite distinct kinds although the islands are comparatively close to each other.

If the early accounts can be believed, several Caribbean islands had macaws. There can be little doubt that these large, noisy super-parrots were endemic on some, but how these forms differed from one another cannot be answered with any degree of accuracy. Walter Rothschild had to assess the veracity of the descriptions when he was compiling his book about extinct birds; he erred on the generous side and gave specific status to many of the Caribbean varieties. For instance, a deep-violet macaw which the natives called *one couli* was reported on Guadeloupe. Although Rothschild named it *Anodorhynchus purpurascens*, the birds were probably hyacinth macaws brought over from Brazil. Red parrots 'as big as chickens' were reported on Guadeloupe in April 1496 by Christopher Columbus; the natives called these birds *guacamayos*. In support of this, a large red and yellow macaw was reported living on the same island in 1667, to which was assigned the name *Ara guadeloupensis*. There is credible evidence that such a bird may also have occurred on Martinique and Dominica. As there are no skins to examine, verification of this 'species' is impossible. Green and yellow macaws lived on Dominica, according to Thomas Atwood who wrote a general account of the island in 1791. He stated that they were plentiful and made a disagreeable noise. The 'species' is called *Ara atwoodi*. Another similar looking bird occurred on Jamaica, which Rothschild called *A. erythrocephala*. Could these mythical macaws refer to *A. militaris*, the military macaw of Mexico which was either living naturally in the Caribbean or had established itself from birds imported by the local people. Apparently, skins once existed of Dominican and Jamaican macaws, though these went missing some time ago before their status could be confirmed. But a foot-bone of a macaw was found in the remains of a fire on the island of St Croix, and this is the sole clue to the existence of yet another Caribbean species, *Ara autochthones*. However, of one extinct species, there is no doubt – the Cuban red macaw, *Ara tricolor*.

Although it was only two-thirds the size of the largest mainland macaws, the red macaw was a spectacular scarlet bird with an area of yellow on the back of the neck and indigo-blue wings. All the reliable records come from Cuba, where it was probably never numerous, at least in historical times. Red macaws were generally seen in pairs or families, and nested in holes in palm trees. Their diet was fruit and seeds. The natives hunted the birds for their meat, and took the young birds as house pets. By the middle of the last century, the birds were confined to the Zapata Swamp on the south Cuban coast. The last one seen there was shot in 1864, though possibly a few may have escaped the attention of the local people for a decade or two. Cuban red macaws certainly survived until the turn of the century in the Berlin zoological gardens, but they were the last of their kind. Only a dozen or so skins remain in museum cabinets as tangible proof of the existence of this lovely macaw.

There is some evidence that the species may have lived on the Isle of Pines and Jamaica. Philip Gosse, the Victorian naturalist who travelled in the Caribbean, saw a mounted 'red macaw' which was alleged to have been shot on Jamaica in 1765. It certainly had the characteristic colouring of the Cuban species, but was later named by Rothschild *Ara gossei*. On the other hand, it is known that the people of Jamaica frequently imported scarlet macaws (*Ara macao*) from South America. Even so, perhaps the Cuban red macaw did live as a wild endemic bird in the central mountains of Jamaica. We will never know.

DISAPPEARING AMAZONS

Human settlement in the Caribbean did not leave the amazons unscathed. Of the 11 or so species that used to live in the West Indies, 2 have become extinct. One that lived on Guadeloupe was probably a gorgeous bird, if the description of Du Tertre can be taken at face value. Writing in the seventeenth century, he said this parrot was the size of a hen, the eyes and beak were bordered with red, much of the body plumage was coloured violet, shot with green and black, changing 'like the throat of a pigeon'. Furthermore, it could, like so many amazons, raise the iridescent neck feathers to create a frilled collar, framing the head. The Guadeloupe amazon must have resembled the scarce green and purple imperial parrot or *sisserou* of the mountain forests of Dominica. Being comparatively flat, Guadeloupe was settled and farmed more intensively than other islands in the Lesser Antilles, and these parrots could not withstand the destruction of the forests where they lived. The French immigrants and the African slaves brought in to work the plantations needed protein, and parrots were as good as pigeon to eat. Doubtless persistent persecution of parrots for the table was a contributory cause of the rapid extirpation of the violet amazon (*Amazona violacea*) from Guadeloupe early in the eighteenth century, and very similar looking birds from the neighbouring island of Martinique at about the same time.

Considering the scale of human settlement on the Caribbean islands, with the accompanying destruction of the forests, it is perhaps a wonder that any amazon parrots survive there at all. Although the large amazons of the Lesser Antilles are in a parlous state (see Chapter 6), the smaller green species are still fairly numerous. The only casualty among them is the Puerto Rican amazon, a handsome emerald-green species with a ruby forehead and white 'spectacles', which remains critically endangered in the rainforest on the Luquillo Mountains to the north-east of the island. The sub-species that was once confined to the island of Culebra has not been seen since 1899 when the amazons on the main island of Puerto Rico were still plentiful. The latter densely populated island also lost its Hispaniola conures, as did Mona Island. The small green parrots may have been exterminated as a result of suffering heavy casualties during pigeon shoots. However, the species still survives on Hispaniola, where the pressure of human settlement was originally less severe.

EXTINCTION IN THE PACIFIC

There were once parakeets on Tahiti and Raiatea. It is difficult to imagine a more remote part of the Pacific to be invaded by non-migratory land birds, yet evidence suggests that the ancestors of these parrots came perhaps in stages from New Zealand, 3,200km (1,990 miles) to the south-west, where their closest relatives still live.

The medium-sized, green parakeets of the genus *Cyanorhamphus* that used to be widespread in New Zealand were enterprising birds, because over the ages they launched out over the Pacific and, with the wind under their tails, dispersed to many offshore and oceanic islands. They reached New Caledonia, 110km (70 miles) to the north, and to the chilly sub-antarctic outpost of Macquarie Island, 900km (560 miles) to the south. In such places, they evolved into distinct island races. The red-crowned parakeet diversified into no less than 9 sub-species, 2 of which have become extinct. The populations on both Macquarie and Lord Howe Islands were comparatively small and accordingly vulnerable. Those on Lord Howe, lying midway between Australia and New Zealand, were exterminated by settlers by the beginning of this century because they damaged crops. Cats abandoned by people who came to slaughter penguins for oil probably killed the Macquarie Island birds. In the absence of trees, these parakeets nested on the ground under bunches of tussock grass which made them particularly prone to the attention of the deadly felines. With the death of the last Macquarie Island parakeet, perhaps before 1914, the world lost its only sub-antarctic parrot. The most southerly ones in that sector of the planet are on Antipodes Island, a speck of land merely 40km (25 miles) long, situated to the south west of New Zealand. Here a unique sub-species of the red-crowned parakeet coexists with a larger green species, the Antipodes Island parakeet.

Those parakeets that made the astonishing journey to the Society Islands had sufficient time to evolve into quite separate species. However, they remain even today rather enigmatic birds because so little is known about them. They first came to light during the course of Cook's southern explorations. When the *Endeavour* sailed into Matavai Bay in 1769, the crew which had been cooped up on board continuously for eight months found more than voluptuous Polynesian women to excite and delight them. The island of Otaheite, as it was called, was a place of grand beauty. The jungle, split by sparkling cataracts and waterfalls, rose up the sides of high valleys inland until it vanished in clouds billowing up over the central mountain peaks. The people appeared to live well on the benison of sea and land, and made love shamelessly beneath the frangipani blossoms. During their stay, the crew must have seen parrots, although neither Cook nor Sir Joseph Banks mentioned them in their published diaries for this trip. However, Sydney Parkinson, a member of the expedition, made a drawing of a parakeet from the island which is now held in the British Museum (Natural History) London entitled 'no. 5, Green peroquit, Otahite, Aa'; the Aa refers to the Polynesian name for the bird. On the second visit in 1773, George Forster the German naturalist saw parakeets coloured green with red flecks, which were 'numerous'. The Tahitians kept some of these in their homes and 'were very pleased to have their red feathers'. Specimens were obtained and brought back to England, and on the basis of these John Latham described the bird in his *A General Synopsis of Birds* (1781) as *Psittacus* [now *Cyanoramphus*] *zealandicus* – the black-fronted parakeet.

By comparison with the red-crowned parakeets, the birds from Tahiti were rather dull, the crimson replaced by brownish red. The forehead was black or very dark brown, thus its name, and the green plumage was somewhat less vivid, tending towards bluish or grey green. The precise plumage coloration is a little difficult to determine today because of the paucity of material evidence. Two skins survive intact at the Merseyside County Museum, Liverpool, one of which is thought to have belonged to Sir Joseph Banks's collection and may be the bird that Latham examined as his type specimen. The British Museum (Natural History), London, and the Museum National d'Histoire Naturelle, Paris, possess one each. The French skin was the last one to be taken on Tahiti, in 1844.

By that time, the Arcadian society discovered by Cook was corrupt beyond recovery; venereal disease and tuberculosis were rife, and the native people had developed a huge dependency upon alcohol. The endemic wildlife had also suffered under the 'fatal impact' of the Europeans. Not only mariners had gone ashore; so had rats that infested the ships. Cook left cats, which promptly turned their attention to the birds whose responses to such efficient predators had become slack on these tropical havens. Of 16 kinds of birds special to the Society Islands, no less than 6 were exterminated including the black-fronted parakeet which was not observed after 1844. The Society parakeet disappeared even earlier than that.

The Society parakeet as a species is shrouded in mystery because it is known only from two specimens obtained on Raiatea, an island located 320km (200 miles) west of Tahiti. They reveal that the birds differed from other *Cyanoramphus* parakeets in their brownish plumage and yellowish-green underparts. Cook probably brought them back to England after his third trip to the South Seas because he landed on Raiatea on 3 November 1777 and stayed for three months. One is held in the British Museum, another is deposited in Sir John Ashton's Lever Museum, London. The latter specimen was seen by John Latham who called it the Society parrot. There is no other record of this brown parrot ever being seen alive again.

Tahiti lost another species, although it may possibly still exist elsewhere in the Pacific as an imperilled parrot. George Forster was the first to record this beautiful, sapphire-blue parrot which he observed 'on the top of the highest coconut palms' – a reference to the blue or Tahitian lorikeet. This species was formerly distributed not only in the Society Islands, but also across the islands of the Tuomotu Archipelago and the Cook Islands. The spread of the predatory swamp harrier and avian malaria have been blamed for the sad decline of this striking dark-blue parrot with white cheeks and red bill.

Some authorities treat the New Caledonia lorikeet as extinct. This species is known only from two specimens, both hens, collected in 1859 and one of which has been lost. Observations made by an experienced bushman just over a decade ago indicate that there may still be a few of these lorikeets west of Mount Panie. Even so, this lorikeet is either extinct, or on the brink.

THE PARADISE LOST?

Australia has lost only one kind of parrot, but unfortunately it may well have been the loveliest of them all. The paradise parakeet was discovered by John Gilbert, the greatest of all collectors, when he was earning £100 a year in the employ of John Gould. In a letter dated 8 June 1844, Gilbert reported that while he was working in the Darling Downs, Queensland, he had chanced upon a completely new parrot 'without exception, the most beautiful of the whole tribe I have ever yet seen in Australia; the mingling of the beautiful shades of green is its most conspicuous and beautiful character'. He could have continued to wax lyrically about its scarlet shoulders and vent, and azure-blue rump. He then asked his employer to name it after him as *Platycercus gilberti*. It would have been a fitting tribute to his importance to Australian ornithology; for the last five years he had been tramping the bush and had discovered forty species new to science for which Gould took the credit using, almost verbatim, Gilbert's own descriptions. Gould did not comply with the request, and called the parakeet *Platycercus pulcherrimus*, meaning 'very pretty parrot'. Gilbert never received the disappointing news because at the end of June 1845, while on an expedition to the far north of Queensland, he was speared to death by aboriginals.

The paradise parakeet occurred across a swathe of eastern Queensland south to the north-east corner of New South Wales. Gilbert himself noted its behaviour. 'It is, in habits, truly a grass eating Parrot assembling in small families, and feeding in high grass. All specimens I have killed had their stomach-crops fully distended with grass seeds exclusively.' These birds also had the unusual tendency to place their nests inside the mounds of termites. Their breathtaking coloration may have partly caused their downfall.

During the second half of the eighteenth century, these pretty little parakeets were in great demand by the cage-bird trade, and many were caught and sent to London where they were called 'paradise parakeets' because their plumage was 'out of this world'. This was ironical because, as the century wore on, the birds were clearly being driven off the planet by profligate trapping, egg collecting and the changes brought about to the bush by pastoral development. By 1890, the export of the parakeets had ceased, although birds were still offered for sale in Brisbane at 5s a pair. Then, between 1893 and 1902, a series of severe droughts gripped Queensland causing appalling loss of livestock and wildlife. Bush fires ravaged the vegetation, and afterwards paradise parakeets had vanished from their former haunts. It was feared that these exquisites had gone forever.

In 1918 Alec Chisholm, an Australian ornithologist, appealed in the press for information which might lead to the rediscovery of the missing species. He received several reports, many of which referred to earlier sightings. Two seemed reliable and gave him cause for hope. Then, in December 1921, he was contacted by a naturalist-photographer, C. H. Jerrard, who reported seeing seven or eight adults and some young ones on the Upper Burnett River valley, Queensland. He was able to track down their nest in a termite mound, build a hide, and take a series of remarkable stills of the parakeets at their nest. Sadly, the eggs portrayed inside the mound proved to be infertile.

Alec Chisholm was able to confirm Jerrard's observation in that secluded part of Queensland, and was one of the last to witness paradise parakeets in the flesh. Since then, there have been several tantalizing but unsubstantiated observations which keep alive the possibility that somewhere in some remote part of this huge and under-populated continent, these pretty birds are still at large. One factor raises the level of optimism. Australia has quite a track record of 'lost' species being found again. The noisy scrub bird vanished in 1889, only to reappear in 1961; two kinds of grass wrens thought to be extinct were tracked down in the 1960s. Night parrots disappeared sometime after 1912 when the only twentieth-century specimen was taken but these aberrant birds were identified in 1979 at Cooper's Creek, South Australia[*]. Could the pattern be repeated with the paradise parakeet?

There is one potential source of confusion. Aviculturists occasionally claim that stocks of paradise parakeets exist in captivity, and birds said to belong to this species are occasionally offered for sale. These are invariably hybrids between golden-shouldered and mulga parakeets, the cocks of which do bear a strong resemblance to paradise parakeets. This in turn has led to the suggestion that the latter are nothing more than natural hybrids between the two species. The hens provide the crucial evidence against this theory, because the coloration of the hybrid female is quite different from that of the hen paradise parakeet. Only time will tell whether Gould's 'very pretty parrot' is lost forever. However, as we see in the next chapter, there are many species which are still with us but for which time is rapidly running out; they are in peril.

[*] In October 1989 the Australian Geographical Society offered a reward of A$50,000 for acceptable scientific evidence that the night parrot still exists.

The last Spix's Macaw!

6 · PARROTS IN PERIL

A TALE OF TWO PARROTS

In March 1987, five patrol cars carrying twenty policemen screeched to a halt outside a house in Asuncion belonging to a Paraguayan smuggler. They had been tipped off about the presence inside of illegal contraband. Armed with warrants, they made a thorough search and eventually found what they were looking for huddled inside a suitcase – not bags of cocaine, but a pair of barely fledged young parrots worth more than their weight in gold. They were Spix's (little blue) macaws and possibly the last of their kind to have been bred in the wild.

To aviculturists, Spix's is the Rolls Royce of macaws. Although only two-thirds the length of the hyacinth macaw, it is a pretty species, generally rich blue, but lighter on the head, tinged with green or grey. Restricted to the burity-palm swamps of Curaca, Bahia, in north-east Brazil where it was discovered in 1819 by the German zoologist, Johann Baptist von Spix, these macaws were probably never particularly numerous. Unfortunately, rarity and beauty are qualities for which collectors will pay handsomely, so despite the fact that the birds were 'protected', they were still keenly sought by trappers.

Profit is what motivated the Brazilian poacher who bribed a park guard to turn a blind eye while he shinned up a hollow palm and stole this brood of Spix's macaws during February 1987. The exercise was well worth his while because, within a day or two, he sold them to a dealer in São Paulo for $10,000; the latter, in turn, smuggled them into Paraguay where he doubled his investment. The person who bought the two young macaws for $20,000 looked to Europe for a client. In Asuncion, he forged documents, claiming that the birds were reared in the city zoo so that he could 'legally' export them to Switzerland where an importer was willing to pay $40,000 on expectation of selling them on to a collector for perhaps twice this figure. Unfortunately, the Paraguayan dealer's plans were dashed when the Swiss importer decided to check that he could legally receive a pair of these exceptionally rare macaws. The secretariat of the Convention on International Trade in Endangered Species of Wild Fauna and Flora (CITES), based in Lausanne, was alerted by the enquiry and set into train an international rescue operation resulting in the police swoop. The birds were granted asylum in the Brazilian embassy in Paraguay, then extradited to São Paulo, Brazil, where they joined three adults to form the nucleus for a breeding programme to try and restore the fortunes of this severely endangered species. The people in charge of the project will need a great deal of luck because there may be none left in the wild and only about 40 remain in captivity scattered in collections around the world. The fate of this beautiful parrot therefore depends upon the initiative of a few people who own the last Spix's macaws. At the time of writing, there is unfortunately little sign that the cooperation so desperately needed between owners is forthcoming.

A WORLD PROBLEM

Spix's macaw is, however, by no means the rarest or most threatened parrot in the world.

In 1988, the International Council for Bird Preservation (ICBP) produced a book called *Birds to Watch.* The simplicity of its title belied its stark message. The publication was a global overview of threatened birds, and the facts and figures buried in the text made sobering reading.

Of 9,000 or so kinds of birds known to science, no less than 1,000 are to a varying degree at risk of extinction. This reflects a rapid deterioration of the planet's natural habitats, with the greatest effects being felt in the tropics; Brazilian and Indonesian birds are suffering particularly badly with 121 and 126 threatened species respectively. Parrots are depressingly well represented in this catalogue of gloom, with 71 in peril. No less than 45 of the 145 kinds of parrots that occur between Mexico and Argentina are endangered. As a proportion of the 333 species of parrots, the number at risk is appallingly high. The reasons are trapping for the cage-bird trade and deforestation. Alas, we are the culprits.

THE CONQUEST OF THE FORESTS

Most parrots live in lowland, tropical forests, and these are being cleared at a frightening rate. Anyone who has flown over the tropics will have seen the persistent pall of smoke which all too often signifies forests on the wane. In those places, parrots are being deprived of their homes and livelihoods.

Such evergreen forests can occur anywhere between the Tropics of Cancer and Capricorn where the temperature is relatively high and the rainfall sufficient to promote lush vegetation. Today, they blanket about 7 per cent of the world's surface, but support nearly 50 per cent of the planet's species. Even Christopher Columbus was impressed by the diversity of trees he saw on Hispaniola; they were 'so tall that they seemed to touch the sky, green and lovely, some of them flowering, some bearing fruit, and some at another stage according to their nature'. We know today that a single hectare (2.5 acres) of this rich arboreal growth may include a hundred kinds of trees each with its own interdependent fauna and flora. Many of the plants have already bequeathed to us valuable food and drugs, and doubtless many more harbour pharmacological treasures of potential benefit to mankind. Even the Amazonian burity palm, often associated with Spix's macaw, synthesises large quantities of vitamins A and C. Indeed, the business of cataloguing what lives in these equatorial forests is still far from complete; if a raucous bird like the El Oro parakeet can remain unknown until a decade ago, then clearly cohorts of invertebrates and plants must be waiting to be found. Some scientists believe that the number may run into tens of millions. Unfortunately, species are disappearing faster than they can be found and properly described, because the forests are diminishing year by year.

A few thousand years ago, tropical rainforests covered 14 per cent of the globe, so we have already made substantial inroads into this precious habitat. Most of the damage has been inflicted over the last two centuries, but with a vengeance since World War II. The damage varies from country to country. Only half the original forest cover is left in Latin America; South East Asia and the Pacific islands have retained 25 per cent; West Africa has retained only 18 per cent. However, mainland India, Haiti and Sri Lanka have felled all their virgin rainforest, and within a short time the lowland forests will have vanished from the Philippines, Guatemala, Panama, Sierra Leone, the Ivory Coast and the peninsula part of Malaysia and Thailand. Significant tracts of pristine forest still exist in 37 countries, although 3 account for half the total; Brazil boasts the lion's share of one-third, with Zaire and Indonesia possessing one-tenth each. Nevertheless, the speed with which rainforests are being felled is giving cause for concern. According to one United Nations' survey, some 6 million ha (23,000 sq miles) are disappearing before the chain-saws every year – an area equivalent to West Virginia or Ireland. To put this figure in more manageable terms, 12ha (30 acres) are destroyed every minute of every day. There are even more pessimistic estimates. In 1980, the US National Academy of Sciences announced that an area the size of England, Scotland and Wales – 20 million ha (50 million acres) – is felled or seriously degraded each year. Why?

The current burning of the Brazilian rainforest to make pasture has been called the greatest environmental folly ever to be unleashed on earth. But the fires are often stoked in part by western investment. What starts with the chain-saw ends up as minced beef for fast foods in North America; it takes 5m² (55sq ft) of forest to make a single hamburger. Sadly, the soil fails disastrously after a few years and is then fit to support only worthless scrub. Timber worth $7 billion annually is also extracted from the forests, much of it going to Japan; diamonds and gold are mined from the ground, and electricity flows from dams that drown great swathes of tropical trees. The rivers of the Amazon Basin are capable of generating 100,000 megawatts – equivalent to an oil well gushing 5 million barrels of oil every day. The scale of forest destruction to achieve this output of power will be 207,000ha (800sq miles) of the Amazon forest; Grenada, Barbados and Martinique would fit comfortably into the reservoir behind the dam. But there may be another reason for flattening the forests, summed up by the slogan of Panama's military rulers – *la conquista de la selva* (the conquest of the forest).

Jungles are slightly daunting places and need taming! Despite the fact that they are bursting with life, even supporting small groups of tribal people and helping to regulate the world's climate, fiscally minded rulers feel uncomfortable with huge areas of 'non-productive' land on their doorsteps. Their reaction is usually to subjugate and 'improve' it turning the natural resources of the forests into quick profits. Is it to be wondered that the parrots which depend upon such places are under siege?

No parrot which depends upon rainforest will be completely safe until the current spate of destruction ceases, or until sufficiently large refuges are set aside. In Mexico, Colombia, Ecuador and Peru, the clearance of mid-altitude forests has brought thirteen species of parrots to a perilous state, including the recently discovered El Oro parakeet. The tropical forests in Madagascar are being wiped out, and so the survival of the world's dullest parrot, the vasa, must be open to doubt. Once the forests of the Philippines are finally cleared, the endemic cockatoo will go with them. There is no question that several

Caribbean amazons are threatened, not least by tropical cyclones which tear up tracts of forest. In 1988, Hurricane Gilbert devastated Jamaica and the Caymans and damaged forest where four native parrots live. However, the amazons of the Lesser Antilles are most endangered by the pressure of people and their need to harness more land to grow crops.

PRECARIOUS PARROTS OF THE ANTILLES

Like most of the larger parrots, adult amazons are long lived, slow to mature, and not particularly prolific breeders, so they are unable to adjust to a rapid loss of tree cover. If the birds are persecuted and trapped as well, the population does not easily recover. In the case of the imperial amazon, one of the most severely threatened of American parrots, there were only 150 left in Dominica in 1978 when the ICBP made its first checklist of rare birds; now, there are less than 50 which have to share the island with 85,000 land-hungry people. Furthermore, it is almost impossible to guarantee their protection. Hurricanes are an ever present threat, and have already wiped out one population; and the relentless conversion of primary forest into banana plantations has brought the numbers to a dangerously low level. Those that survive are confined, with the more numerous red-necked amazon, to the region of Morne Diablotin and the Picard River. Although a national park has been established at Morne Anglaise, it is doubtful whether any of these large parrots live within its boundary.

However, the situation is not totally without hope. In October 1986, parrot enthusiasts meeting at Loro Parque, Tenerife, for the First International Parrot Convention, clubbed together and raised $22,000 to fund research into the life-style and requirements of the two beautiful Dominican amazons. The money was donated to the ICBP to administer. One priority is to start an educational programme to win the hearts and minds of local people so that they will come to value their natural heritage. By focusing on the plight of the imperial parrot, they hope to develop a plan to protect and manage the bird's last refuge. Without the support of the Dominican people, the eagle-

Puerto Rican Amazon

Imperial Amazon

Haiti

Dominican Republic

Puerto Rica

St Vincent Amazon

Dominica

St Lucia

St Vincent

St Lucia Amazon

The Rare Caribbean Amazons

like amazon with its iridescent purple plumage will be gone forever by the end of the century.

The spectacular amazons endemic on St Lucia and St Vincent are more numerous, but they are still considered to be in a precarious state. Both are confined to the vestigial forests in the mountainous centres of these lovely islands. The St Lucia amazon is a gorgeous parrot with verdant-green plumage, scarlet wing flashes and a blue face. It has always been sought after for the pet trade. However, aviculture has provided a stock of these birds as an insurance against the collapse of the population of 300 or so free-flying ones on the island.

In 1975 when the numbers in the wild were down to 100, the St Lucia Government asked the Jersey Wildlife Preservation Trust to collect 7 parrot fledglings from their nests to establish a captive breeding programme in Jersey. It came to fruition 7 years later when the first chick hatched. St Lucia, meanwhile, had gained her independence and the parrot – affectionately called Jacquot – was named as the national bird and officially protected. Since then the numbers in the forests have slowly built up. Paul Butler, an English ornithologist, took the plight of the precious parrots to the schools and ordinary people by means of calypsos and billboards. To date, 14 young Jaquots have been fledged in Jersey and a pair is due to be flown back to St Lucia accompanied by the Prime Minister, Mr John Compton, to start the island's own captive breeding programme.

The St Vincent amazon is that island's national bird. It is a rich tawny parrot with a long, three-barred tail in orange, blue and yellow. When they emerge from the tree canopy into the sun, the back-lighting through the orange wing feathers has been likened to the 'beauty of a stained glass window'. St Vincent amazons have always had to live with natural disasters. On 29 August 1980, Hurricane Allen struck the island and devastated 80 per cent of the forest. Apart from cyclones, volcanic eruptions have added to the toll inflicted on the population by the plundering of nests for youngsters. In 1982, the ICBP and the University of East Anglia mounted an expedition to assess the status of this species. They estimated that 420 or so parrots still lived in about 30sq km (12sq miles) of forest in the centre of the island. A further 23 parrots were in the houses of local people.

Paul Butler, funded by the Philadelphia-based conservation organisation Rare Animals' Relief Effort (RARE), has also started to win the sympathy of the local people for the imperilled parrot, and to use it as the focus of a wider campaign to protect the remaining rainforest. Images of the birds are displayed all over the island on posters, T-shirts and car stickers; a brewery has even put a parrot on the bottles of one of its products. The island's newspaper runs a weekly cartoon showing the adventures of 'Vincey' in its struggle to survive. Butler is also waging his campaign in the schools of St Vincent; the children enthusiastically sing calypsos about the beleaguered birds while his wife dresses up as a pantomime parrot. It's all good fun, but the message strikes home. And concern for the rare birds has led to concern for the health of the environment in general, the coral reefs in particular. Should Jacquot's forest home be destroyed, the reefs will be inundated with silt as the heavy tropical rain removes the soil from the unprotected surface. Butler will shortly start a similar campaign to help the imperial amazon on Dominica.

There are still problems on St Vincent. As many as 30 young parrots are still being taken from their nests every year although it is illegal to own one on the island. However, a breeding programme has been underway for some time. There are at least 100 of these parrots outside St Vincent including some in reputable collections, like the Vogelpark, Walsrode, Germany, and the New York Zoological Society's breeding premises on St Catherine's Island, North Carolina.

If extravagant sums of money are the key to a species' survival, the Puerto Rican amazon should be utterly safe because millions of dollars have been spent to save this endemic parrot. Puerto Rico was in the forefront of those Caribbean islands where settlement and agriculture devastated the covering of trees, three-quarters of it being removed during the second half of the nineteenth century. The plight of the parrot was fundamentally caused by this drastic change of land use, but it has been brought back from the brink of extinction by human intervention on a grand scale. This handsome emerald green species with white spectacles and a ruby-red forehead is the last native parrot remaining on US territory. As the forests were cleared, and selective felling for charcoal of the large Palo Colorado trees in which the birds nested took place, the birds became scarce. The subsequent spread of agriculture caused them to retreat into the mountains. By the 1940s, the amazon's last refuge was 1,620ha (4,000 acres) of the Luquillo Forest, equivalent to 0.2 per cent of their former range. The steepest decline in numbers took place between 1930 and the 1960s, and was brought about by systematic nest robbing; few nestlings fledged during this period. This form of abuse has now been stemmed, although a spirit of lawlessness still prevails on the island.

Little concern was shown for the safety of the parrots until 1953 when Jose Rodriguez-Vidal from Puerto Rico's Department of Agriculture conducted a survey of the remaining 200 or so birds to discover why they were faring so badly. He found that they had a lamentably low breeding success. The 16 nests that he monitored contained 33 eggs, but 8 were infertile, 6 were consumed by rats, and 2 by pearly-eyed thrashers – thrushlike birds with long, sharp beaks. Of 17 that hatched, only 14 fledged. Another census carried out in 1963 revealed that only a scant 130 individuals survived. But further pressures conspired to depress the population yet further. US forces destroyed part of the forest for military exercises, irradiating part of the area and testing noxious herbicides like 'agent orange' before operational deployment in Vietnam. Meanwhile, logging, nest vandalism and disturbance due to the recreational activities in the Caribbean National Forest in the Luquillo Mountains continued unabated. In 1975, only 13 Puerto Rican amazons were left, giving cause for concern.

By then, a determined programme to save the parrot had been mounted by the US Fish and Wildlife Service, the US Forest Service and staff from the Puerto Rico Department of Natural Resources. Using a variety of techniques, the wild population has been slowly restored to just over 30, and a further 37 are at present in captivity. But only 4 pairs are breeding properly and the recruitment of sexually active birds in the population remains mysteriously low.

The slight upward turn in the parrot's fortunes has been achieved by identifying and then eliminating the factors that were depressing the breeding productivity of the free-flying birds. Parrot sleuths from the Wildlife Service discovered that there was a drastic shortage of nest sites, pairs frequently squabbling over holes. In one particularly murderous conflict between two prospecting couples, one bird from each was killed. Many holes were too small or too wet, and of those that were suitable many were already occupied by bees or other kinds of hole-nesting birds. To solve this problem, fifty trees in the Luquillo forest were fitted with nest boxes, custom-built from plastic sewer pipes, each covered with glue and sprinkled with sawdust and moss to blend in with the background. The parrots quickly took to the new accommodation, but so did other birds. Pearly-eyed thrashers competed vigorously with the amazons for nest sites, and occasionally even predated the eggs and chicks. By trying out a variety of different designs, the members of the parrot rehabilitation scheme discovered that nest boxes which were deeply recessed were still acceptable to amazons but not to thrashers. However, the aggressive thrashers had their uses. Special boxes were erected close to the parrot holes so that the parrots could benefit from the spirited way in which their smaller neighbours deterred other 'house-hunting' thrashers.

Other measures included monitoring the chicks for infestation by warble-fly maggots, which insidiously eat their way into the vital organs, but which can be surgically removed if caught in time. Predators were also controlled in the vicinity of the nest sites. Adult red-tailed hawks were removed during the period when the young parrots were fledging, as were rats. Once the youngsters had flown, the entrances to the nests were covered to prevent swarms of bees taking over the accommodation. These techniques helped to boost the breeding success of the amazons from between 11 and 26 per cent prior to 1973, to 70 per cent.

Captive breeding was also part of the strategy for ensuring a future for the Puerto Rican amazon. The first clutches laid by the hens were removed, thus inducing the birds to produce another batch of eggs. The 'surplus' eggs were then incubated by surrogate mothers. With the help of Hispaniolan amazon foster parents, thirty-seven of the endangered species are, as already mentioned, now held in aviaries.

The Puerto Rican amazon programme is not without its difficulties. Several of the females persistently lay infertile eggs; only two are producing viable ones. Although artificial insemination may be a solution to this problem, so far this particular species has proved to be intractable in insemination trials. Another breeding facility is planned for the Abajo State Forest, at a cost of $750,000 over the next year or two, to spread the risk across two populations of these scarce parrots. And yet, in spite of all the money and resources allocated to the project, there are still fewer than 70 Puerto Rican amazons, so they cannot be considered out of danger. This has led to much criticism by those who maintain that the scale of the effort and finance is a reflection of scandalous mismanagement, and point to Paul Butler's achievements on St Vincent with relatively few resources.

REPATRIATED PARROTS

The ultimate objective of all breeding programmes is to act as an insurance scheme should a species become extinct in the wild, and to provide a stock of birds to reintroduce back into the natural habitats when it is deemed safe to do so. This is no substitute for saving and restoring the forests themselves; however, there have been a few attempts to repatriate parrots.

The business of liberating parrots reared in captivity is fraught with difficulties, as an experiment carried out in the Dominican Republic revealed. In 1982, an attempt was made to reintroduce 36 Hispaniolan amazons into a forested area close to the Haitian border; 23 came from the Puerto Rican programme and 13 were donated by the zoo in Santo Domingo. The birds were divided into two flocks, one of which was forcibly released without any preparation. They dispersed immediately, displaying no flock cohesion, and within a few days the birds had lost condition. Quite simply, they did not know how to survive in the wild; many must have sooner or later starved to death or been killed by peasant farmers. The second group coped better. They were initially retained in an aviary in full view of the release area. Furthermore, their diet was supplemented by seeds and fruit that occurred naturally in the surrounding countryside. After a week or two, the doors of the aviary were opened and the birds allowed to go or return as they pleased. These 'educated' amazons tended to stick together around the release site, foraged effectively for food, and eventually integrated into the local parrot population.

Some Puerto Rican amazons bred in captivity have been reintroduced back into the Luquillo Forest, thus augmenting the productivity of the wild birds. One direct release of 3 birds was not an outstanding success because 2 were killed shortly after they gained their freedom. The best method involved placing aviary-bred chicks in the nests of wild birds which then reared them to the point of fledging.

Another scheme is underway to establish thick-billed parrots in Arizona. This predominantly bottle-green parrot lives in the conifer forests of central Mexico where it used to thrive on the seeds of the chihuahua pine. It was once a regular visitor to the south-eastern quarter of Arizona and certain parts of New Mexico. In recent years, considerable logging operations in the Sierra Madre Occidental have reduced the numbers of these fine parrots and they have long since ceased to turn up in the USA. A slight change in forestry practices

Thick-billed Parrots

whereby five mature pine trees are retained in every hectare could safeguard the bird's food and nest sites. Meanwhile, thick-billed parrots bred in captivity have been let loose in an area of Arizona managed in the interests of the birds. So far, the scheme looks promising and may once more establish a wild population of parrots on North American soil.

BRAZILIAN GOLD

Two Brazilian species deserve mention because their scarcity may be due to the destruction of their forested homelands. The golden conure, sometimes called the Queen of Bavaria's conure, possesses dazzling yellow plumage relieved only by dark-green flight feathers and outer wing coverts. It is the largest of the conures and the outsize head and beak make it look rather like a small macaw. This brightly coloured parrot is restricted to a small area of north-east Brazil from the Xingu river, Para, east to western Maranhão, where it is threatened by the development taking place in that part of the Amazon. The conure's country has been violated by two major roads – the Trans-Amazon and the Belem to Brasilia highways – which have razed millions of acres of forest to the ground, bringing development in their wake. The huge Tucurui Dam will inundate vast areas of the forest that fall within the conure's domain. As the outlook appears grim for these parrots, the creation of a secure reserve is a top priority as is the establishment of a captive population of nesting birds. The birds are kept by aviculturists, although they are scarce and thus 'worth their weight in gold'. They have a reputation for playfulness and a 'piercing shriek that can distress a sensitive ear'.

The Brazilian red-tailed amazon is another parrot in peril. The species is limited to a fairly inaccessible area of swampy forest in the south of the state of São Paulo. Little is known about this species because access to the parrot's heartland in the Serra do Mar is through malaria and snake infested country. It nests in dead palm stumps situated in the middle of open marshes. However, the place is not protected from timber exploitation and bird trapping, so a reserve is called for to give these amazons a degree of safety. About 30 are in captivity in Brazil, but this number is insufficient to ensure survival.

ANOTHER EXTINCTION ON MAURITIUS?

Island species, especially those confined to single, small islands are particularly precarious because the populations are often relatively small. The number of birds threatened with extinction reflects the fragile nature of island forms; according to the ICBP, 473 are currently in a perilous state. Apart from the Caribbean amazons and Spix's macaw, the Mauritius parakeet may be the most endangered parrot in the world, and we may be too late to save it.

These pretty green 'ring-necks' were once common on Mauritius and Reunion. Deforestation and shooting exterminated the birds of Reunion by 1800, but they were still very much in evidence on Mauritius until the beginning of the twentieth century. In 1886, the

Mauritius Parakeet
gazumped by Hill Mynahs

endemic bird had competition for nest sites from introduced ring-necked parakeets from Africa. Later, Indian mynahs joined the fray. By 1982, there were only a dozen or so left, and these were not nesting successfully so the time had come for drastic action if the birds were not to follow the dodo.

Mauritius has been the focus of international concern for some time, and concerted efforts have been made to save the pathetic remnants of the island's endemic wildlife. An important part of the strategy was to establish captive breeding programmes for the particularly vulnerable species which included certain reptiles and fruit bats as well as birds. In 1979 Carl Jones, a Welsh ornithologist and aviculturist, was appointed to the Mauritius Wildlife Research and Conservation Programme. Jones applied himself to the plight of the pink pigeon. Over-zealous hunting, loss of tree cover and cyclone damage had reduced their numbers to a mere 18 in 1984, and all of them were nesting in one grove of trees. However, Jones built up a good breeding group in aviaries and produced about 100 birds; some were even released back into the semi-protected botanic gardens in Pamplemousses. His single-minded devotion to saving rare birds may also have paid off with the Mauritius kestrel which, in the 1970s, was on the verge of extinction with a population of less than 10 individuals.

However, Carl Jones may have come on the scene too late to restore the flagging fortunes of the Mauritius parakeet. Today, only 5 males and 3 females remain in the wild although their last refuge, the Machabee Nature Reserve, is well protected. In 1987, one adult was trapped to found a breeding colony, but sadly it died. However, in December that year, a wild pair produced a pair of youngsters. Their progress was monitored and it was decided that their parents were not giving them sufficient nourishment. They were therefore taken into care and given to a pair of captive ring-necked parakeets to foster. The two birds will be kept in captivity and given every inducement to breed. Future plans for the conservation of the world's scarcest parrot included efforts to broaden the diet of the free-flying birds which tend

Seed killers; double-eyed fig parrots feeding on figs in Indonesia (Jean-Paul Ferrero/Ardea London Ltd)

to rely upon a few endemic plant species. However, only time will tell whether help has arrived too late to save the Mauritius parakeet. If so, it will certainly be the next parrot casualty to qualify for inclusion in Chapter 5.

TEST-TUBE PARROTS

A technique pioneered at London Zoo on budgerigars may come to the rescue of parrots in plight. The experiment carried out by Jaime Samour involved vasectomising a cock budgie with surgical instruments designed for eye operations, and fertilizing his mate, a blue hen called Claudette, with frozen semen donated by another bird. The vasectomy did nothing to reduce the cock budgie's libido. By his constant courting, he brought his mate into breeding fettle but was utterly unable to fertilize her. This was achieved by inseminating her with sperm from a green cock stored at $-196°C$ ($-356°F$) for several weeks. Proof of the successful fertilization was revealed when the two chicks, Frosty and Icy, grew green feathers, thus becoming the first test-tube budgies.

With the increasing stocks of rare parrots in captivity, the transportation of deep-frozen semen around the world may be one method of ensuring a good mixing of genes and preventing undue inbreeding. Parrots reluctant to mate may also be force fertilized using Samour's technique.

KAKAPO AND KILLER CATS

The catastrophic effect of predators and the importance of controlling them is revealed by the quest to save New Zealand's flightless parrot, the kakapo*. One of New Zealand's prehistoric birds, unfortunately it is also one of its most threatened. With no terrestrial predators to cope with, the ancestors of these parrots became heavy, flightless and virtually defenceless. While New Zealand remained a series of island

*Kakapo is a Maori word which takes no 's' in the plural.

Parrots as decoration; this ceremonial head-dress is worn by a man from Mount Hagen, New Guinea, and contains a 'crown' of long-tailed Papuan lorikeets (Author)

havens isolated from the rest of the world, kakapo were safe. They were common throughout the forests which blanketed the countryside. However, the arrival of the Polynesians in AD 750, and later the Europeans, put their survival in jeopardy. Their numbers started to plummet, and today there are barely 50 birds which exist in special sanctuaries managed by the Department of Conservation. It is nothing short of a miracle that any survive at all.

The Polynesian settlers took a shine to kakapo. Being large birds that boomed in the night, the parrots drew attention to themselves. They were also tasty and were hunted by the Maori both to eat and for their skins which were in demand for making capes worn over the shoulder called *kahu kakapo*. Over the course of 1,000 years, the Maori burnt off 23 per cent of the native forest, exterminating at least 38 kinds of birds, including all the moa, pelicans and a variety of

waterfowl, birds of prey and rails. For those, like kakapo, that survived, the amount of habitat available was greatly diminished. Their decline was accelerated by the Europeans who cleared much of the remaining forest to make way for farms, and who also unleashed an unholy alliance of creatures to the detriment of the trusting native birds. Foremost among them was the deadliest of killers, the domestic cat. Its prowess as a catcher of small rodents and birds is recognised by all who keep them as pets, but when loosed into the New Zealand countryside their impact was devastating. In the early 1880s, ferrets, stoats and weasels were also liberated in thousands to combat the plague of rabbits which was despoiling the pastoral lands. Alas, the alien predators were ineffective at controlling their intended prey and turned on the birds instead. During this later period of settlement, a further 20 endemic birds vanished, thereby revealing their naked vulnerability. Surprisingly, the kakapo survived this onslaught – just!

By the middle of the nineteenth century, kakapo were eliminated from North Island, and soon afterwards rapidly disappeared from the low parts of South Island. However, the birds clung to the steeper and more remote parts in the south, where inclement weather slowed the implacable spread of the colonists and their feral animals. Even in 1880, the terrestrial parrots were so common in Fiordland that expeditions into that region could be fed by sending dogs to collect kakapo. As Andreas Reischek, an explorer, noted:

> The birds used to be in dozens around the camp, screeching and yelling like a lot of demons, and at times it was impossible to sleep for the noise. The dog had to be tied up or matters would have been worse. It would have been killing and fetching all night long . . .

But soon, even travellers to the remote wet forests of South Island were recording the dearth of kakapo. Prowling cats and mustelids were picking off the vulnerable parrots while they rested by day or incubated their eggs. The young, of course, were totally defenceless. It seemed that nothing could save them from inevitable extinction. But there was a glimmer of hope in the form of an immigrant naturalist of Irish extraction.

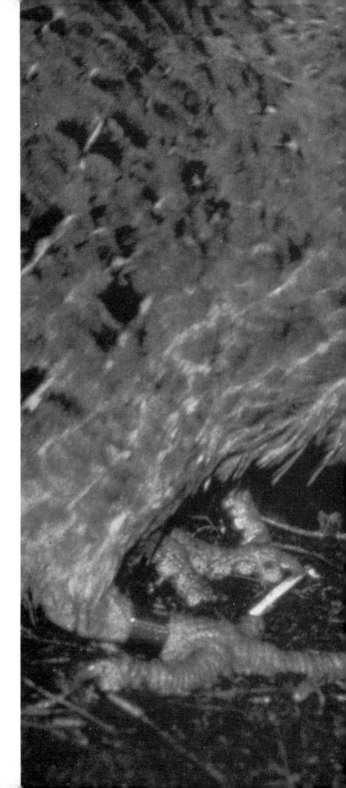

Male kakapo nestling about ten weeks old soliciting food from its mother at nest on Stewart Island on 8 June 1981. This is the first and only time a parent and chick has been observed or photographed together at a nest. The juvenile Snark was transferred to Little Barrier Island in 1982 and the mother Alice to Codfish Island in 1988 (Don Merton)

In 1894, Richard Henry was appointed curator of Resolution Island, a remote place in Dusky Sound, that had been nominated nearly twenty years previously as a penal sanctuary. Criminals were never sent there, but in 1891 the island was reserved for endangered animals and plants. Henry was aware of the wholesale destruction of New Zealand's natural heritage, and had the foresight to see that such predator-free islands could be used as 'arks' for birds like the kakapo which seemed destined for extinction on the mainland. With remarkable industry, he shifted hundreds of native birds of all kinds to Resolution for safe keeping. However, in 1900 he discovered a 'weasel' on the island; his charges were no longer safe. He then moved the birds to smaller islands within Dusky Sound, and to Little Barrier Island, a reserve north-east of Auckland, that had been purchased by the Crown in 1894 and declared a wildlife sanctuary. In fact, cats had already reached Little Barrier, and were not finally eradicated until 1980 by the New Zealand Wildlife Service (now the Department of Conservation), thus restoring it as a safe refuge for 16 kakapo.

After Henry's pioneering work, interest in the kakapo lay fallow until the 1950s when staff from the Wildlife Service made a concerted effort to determine whether viable populations existed in the rugged wooded valleys around Milford Sound. Some were discovered, and an attempt was made to establish a captive breeding programme at Mount Bruce, just north of Wellington. Five were captured, but all eventually died and proved to be males. Over the years, several little groups of kakapo were found in Fiordland, but today only 5 cock birds are known to live in that bleak part of New Zealand. However, virtually unknown to anyone, a more healthy population survived on Stewart Island, at the southern end of South Island.

Although there are few historical reports of kakapo on Stewart Island, they must have been fairly numerous until quite recently. Indeed, in 1949 a deer hunter caught one, and had to offer a few plucked feathers as evidence to be believed. However, in 1977, funds were made available to enable the Wildlife Service to survey fresh areas for kakapo. Surprisingly, between 100 and 200 birds were discovered in the south-east part of the island. As there were females, the scientists were able to study the kakapo's unusual sex life and its ecological

The Kakapo's Last Refuges

Little Barrier Island

NEW ZEALAND

Stewart Island

Codfish Island

requirements. Some kakapo were even named; under scientific observation one called Alice reared a chick which was subsequently named Snark. A film was even made by Television New Zealand's Natural History Unit documenting the male's astonishing courtship and the female's nesting behaviour; Rob Brown's photography will stand as an enduring record of this unique parrot, and may never be repeated. But subsequent surveys revealed that the newly discovered population of parrots was in decline. Once again, deadly cats were to blame. Some people even thought the scientists themselves were blazing trails to the defenceless parrots which the cats then followed. There was certainly cause for concern; 10 cat-ravaged corpses were found one year, and half the kakapo that bore identification marks to help the field biologists in their work were slaughtered between 1977 and 1982. Something had to be done. In a desperate bid to avert disaster, 18 kakapo were moved to Little Barrier Island, now cleared of cats. A campaign of shooting, poisoning and trapping was also waged against feral cats in the kakapo country of Stewart Island. Twenty-nine kakapo were saved (4 females and 25 males). The first batch of 16 birds has already been moved to Codfish Island, another tiny sanctuary off the north-west coast of Stewart Island, from which Australian possums and predatory wekas had to be exterminated.

Much has now been learned of the kakapo's requirements and the knowledge will be applied to prevent these flightless parrots becoming lost forever. Certainly, they cannot coexist with cats, rats or mustelids like stoats, so their refuges must be kept totally free from these creatures. Since Little Barrier and Codfish Islands are virtually the only locations free from such killers in the whole of New Zealand and her 700 offshore islands, the kakapo have nowhere else to go. But these birds have also evolved themselves into a corner by needing specific foods to breed successfully. It seems that the erratic nesting is geared to the fruiting of rimu and kahikatea trees. The normal staple diet of the adults is too poor and fibrous for growing young, so these tree-seeds provide the nourishment necessary for bringing the birds into breeding condition and for fuelling the growth of the chicks. However, these trees produce a good yield of seeds only every two or so years, and this is when the cocks make their scrapes and attract the hens with their booming love songs. Although Codfish Island is satisfactorily endowed with vegetation ideal for kakapo, Little Barrier has relatively few rimu trees. The kakapo settled here therefore face the challenge of having to learn to consume different kinds of food.

In March, 1989, only 40 are known to exist – one solitary cock on Stewart Island, 14 on Little Barrier (8 cocks, 6 hens) and 25 on Codfish Island (20 cocks and 5 hens). However, the New Zealand Department of Conservation has just launched a project with the aim of increasing their numbers to 500, with a fund of 2.5 million NZ$. The project is being led by Don Merton.

BURNING FOR CONSERVATION

'Gardening' on a grand scale may be the key to the survival of two little parakeets in Australia. Regarding the first of these, Melbourne's great sewage farm at Werribee offers a rich experience to visitors during the southern winter. Apart from the presence of large numbers of waders and wildfowl feeding in acre upon acre of sludge settlement lagoons, it is possible to glimpse a few of Australia's most threatened parrots fossicking on the saltmarshes. Slightly larger than budgerigars, the orange-bellied parakeets are charming green, blue and yellow birds, the cocks sporting a patch of orange on their underparts. Sometimes, about 70 – half the total population – gather here in winter, feeding on the seeds of saltbushes and other native plants.

This parakeet is one of the few really migratory parrots, the last 40 pairs breeding on a coastal strip of wet and windy heathland in the south-west corner of Tasmania. Most of them are concentrated in the vicinity of Port Davey, where they choose to nest in hollow gum trees. By the end of the breeding season, the population has generally increased to between 150 and 200, which then make their way north across the stormy waters of Bass Strait, stopping to feed and rest on King Island. When they reach the mainland, they scatter in small flocks to a number of traditional locations on coastal marshes around southern Victoria and South Australia. Orange-bellied parakeets were never particularly numerous although from time to time they were reported in thousands (eg in the 1830s, 1880s and 1910s). Apart from these

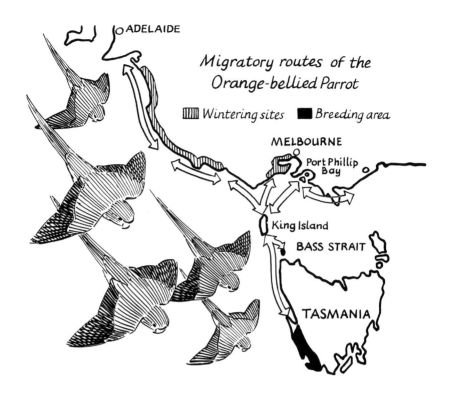

Migratory routes of the
Orange-bellied Parrot

▥ Wintering sites ■ Breeding area

ADELAIDE

MELBOURNE

Port Phillip
Bay

King Island

BASS STRAIT

TASMANIA

periodic irruptions, the population rarely seemed to exceed 1,000. However, a steady decline was noted after World War II, trapping and habitat loss being generally blamed.

Their breeding season in Tasmania coincides with the flowering and seeding of plants in the buttongrass heaths, such as sedges, boronias and a certain kind of everlasting daisy. The mix of vegetation favoured by the birds is transitory and produced by fire. However, the parakeet's diet varies with time. When the birds arrive in October, they devour the seeds of sedges growing on land that was consumed by flames between seven and ten years previously; later in the season they transfer to vegetation on more recently burnt areas. Fire is, and always has been, a powerful force in the shaping of Australian vegetation. It was particularly favoured by the Aborigines who frequently set alight tracts of countryside in order to destroy rank vegetation that impeded movement, and to encourage a fresh flush of grass for attracting wombats and wallabies which they hunted. In the coastal areas of

Tasmania, the periodic use of the 'fire stick' also benefited the orange-bellied parakeets because it encouraged their favourite food plants to appear a few years after the flames had killed the foliage.

Today, controlled burning is used to maintain plant diversity, thus creating a mosaic of suitable areas that cater for the tastes of these scarce parakeets. Care has to be taken, however, to preserve patches of forest and melaleuca scrub that the birds use for roosting and nesting. The Tasmanian National Parks and Wildlife Service implements the pattern of burning and has been rewarded for its pains. A parrotless area which was set alight for the first time after 23 years supported 3-4 nesting pairs of parakeets 3 years later. There is an added advantage to burning small patches in rotation because it prevents the vegetation of large areas becoming uniformly rank with the attendant risk of causing huge bush fires. This happened in 1986 when 20,000ha (50,000 acres) were reduced to ashes, depriving 10 pairs of orange-bellied parakeets of nesting sites and rendering the area unsuitable for a further two years. The wintering habitats also appear to be in need of restoration.

A careful study of their winter diet at Werribee revealed that, for a period, the parakeets preferred the nourishing seeds of goosefoot, a native weed that contaminated the Italian rye grass employed by the sewage works for drawing off nutrients from the waste slurry. Unfortunately, the 'parrot-friendly' weed was confined to comparatively small areas of the filtration paddocks; on suitable ground elsewhere the plant was smothered by another aggressive grass from Europe. Although the parakeets still tackled the alien grass seeds, they much preferred those of the Australian species.

For a long time, it was assumed that the demise of the orange-bellied parakeet had been caused by large-scale industrial development of its coastal wintering places, especially around Phillip Bay, south of Melbourne. But it is also possible that the changes to the vegetation due to the spread of alien plants contributed to the parakeet's decline. However, now that the requirements of the birds are better understood, the information can be used to rehabilitate the saltmarshes. But the parakeets are still under threat from further loss of habitat, most critically from the area fringing the lagoons around Point Wilson where the majority of the birds spend the winter. This is zoned for yet further industrial development. At the moment, the pretty little parakeets are holding their own and their interests are being well looked after by a recovery team run by the Tasmanian, South Australian and Australian National Parks and Wildlife Services, the Victorian Fisheries and Wildlife Service, and the Royal Australian Ornithologist's Union.

Fire is also a management tool for protecting the ground parrot that was once widespread throughout the coastal heathlands. Two sub-species are recognised, one from eastern Australia and Tasmania, the other from the south-western region of Western Australia. Both suffered significant reductions after Europeans colonized the continent and introduced predators like cats and dogs; trampling by cattle, loss of suitable habitat through draining, and changes in fire regimes also put the parrots in some difficulty. A recent survey indicates that the skulking green parrots are extinct in the western part of their range. However, they are still common in a few isolated pockets in Victoria and New South Wales where they prefer heath with a thick cover of Banksias and casuarinas and a high density of seeding sedges. Periodic burning at the correct frequency is needed to maintain the parrot's habitat at its optimum carrying capacity.

In temperate shrubby heaths, the ground parrots recolonize areas 3-4 years after they have been burnt, and rapidly increase to maximum density after a further 2-3 years; thereafter the numbers fall until, after 20 years, all the birds have departed. In places managed for ground parrots, patches of heathland are set alight once every 15-20 years to maintain ideal conditions.

COCKATOOS UNDER PRESSURE

Species often come under pressure long before they reach dangerously low population levels, and become of concern to conservationists. Some of the cockatoos of Western Australia are showing signs of stress as a result of the way settlers have altered the vegetation.

Nine kinds of cockatoo inhabit the south-west corner of Western Australia; sulphur-crests were introduced during the 1930s but the galahs, corellas, 'blacks' and Major Mitchell's are all native to the region. They have had to weather the human impact on the countryside which has turned it into the 'wheat belt' of Australia. The speed with which the landscape has been altered has been astonishingly rapid.

Europeans started to settle in this part of the continent in 1827, but by the end of the century a scattering of homesteads accounted for only 500km² (193sq miles). However, much of the native forest has been felled within living memory. Since 1945, no less than 3,300 new farms have been established, bringing the total land cleared to 130,000sq km (500,000sq miles). In the creation of this agricultural 'prairie', covered with exotic crops and alien grass, little space was reserved for the indigenous vegetation. A few areas have been designated National Parks and Nature Reserves (2 per cent of the total area), State Forests (4 per cent) and some remain vacant Crown land (18 per cent) and as shelters around buildings and paddocks. The cockatoos, which are utterly dependent upon the native plants, have suffered as a result of this spread of agriculture. The short-billed, white-tailed black cockatoo is one such species. It never took to cereals, and to this day prefers to feed primarily on the seeds of local proteas. The extent of the human impact on these lordly birds was revealed in a comparative study of two breeding populations, one at Coomallo Creek, where there was extensive native vegetation, the other at Manmanning where little indigenous plant cover remained.

The breeding productivity and the effort expended by the parents in the two locations was significantly different. At Coomallo Creek, nearly two-thirds of the pairs produced a single fledgling, while at Manmanning less than one-third of the cockatoo couples successfully reared families. At Coomallo Creek, the parrots were clearly less pressed to find sufficient food for their needs. The hens were fed by their mates during the incubation period; when their chicks arrived the hens brooded them for 21 days, they grew well and fledged at a good weight. By contrast, the Manmanning birds had to struggle; the hens often had to leave their eggs to forage, and ceased daytime brooding the chicks when they were about 10 days old. They were rarely given a mid-morning feed, put on less weight, and fledged lighter than the more 'affluent' birds at Coomallo Creek. The relative wealth of resources at the two sites is indicated by the fact that the Manmanning population was less than one-fifth the size of that of Coomallo Creek (94 pairs as opposed to 400), and yet the birds needed to forage over distances four times greater to obtain sufficient food to meet their needs. Is it to be wondered that these white-tailed black cockatoos died out at Manmanning by 1978?

For some cockatoos, the availability of cereals is nothing short of a bonanza and they have greatly benefited from the transformation of the eucalypt woodlands into grain-producing prairies. Both kinds of corellas, the inland race of the red-tailed black and the galah, avidly devour cereals and agricultural weeds. In particular, the spread of the galah is a great success story. The birds were once confined to water-courses, and foraged on the ground for a variety of seeds. Nowadays, the wheat belt provides the mobs of shocking-pink and grey cockatoos with food galore, with spilled seed from sacks, silos and lorries supplementing the loose grain on the stubble. Even the presence of horses helps the galahs to make a good living. If the beasts are fed on grain much of it passes through their digestive tract intact, and is then picked up as leftovers by the gluttonous parrots. Many farms have established open watering holes for stock and keep a few old trees for shielding animals from the baking-hot sun, and both these have assisted the dramatic spread of galahs in that part of Australia.

But introduced seeds are a mixed blessing for the inland sub-species of the red-tailed black cockatoo. Although northern Australia is the stronghold of these magnificent super-parrots, they reach the south-western corner of the continent. Their favourite food is an alien grass called 'doublegee' (if you happen to stand on the spiky seeds with bare feet, you'll likely yell out 'Gee, Geeee'!). Every square metre of heavily infested ground may contain 9,000 seeds; as a hungry cockatoo can thrive happily on a daily ration of 3,500 seeds, there is thus ample food lying around. This may have been what initially tempted the cockatoos to spread into agricultural areas. The cost to them may be a low breeding rate.

Only one-third of all nesting attempts by this species in this area results in fledged young, and these tend to be underweight, being only 76 per cent the weight of an adult female; a bonny fledgling cockatoo should be nearly as heavy as its mother. Food quality has been suspected for depressing the yield of young parrots. Perhaps the doublegee on which the parents gorge themselves does not provide the nestlings with a good balanced diet. Alternatively, the red-tailed black cockatoos in this part of Australia may be affected by the herbicides which are sprayed onto the seeds, including the weeds, thus resulting in fewer and lighter than normal fledglings.

The lovely Major Mitchell's cockatoo is becoming scarce in settled areas of the bush. Most populations consist of between 50 and 150 birds that tend to coalesce into one or two foraging flocks outside the breeding season. Loss of nest sites caused by the fragmentation and destruction of the native vegetation may be a crucial factor in the decline of this species. This cockatoo's belligerent disposition towards others of its own kind nesting too close exacerbates the situation. Pairs of these pink cockatoos need space and will not tolerate others

A pair of Major Mitchell's Cockatoos survey an area of Western Australia converted to growing wheat.

setting up homes within 2km (1 mile). Even if an isolated block of wood contains sufficient nest holes for 75 pairs, only 1 couple of Major Mitchell's will take up residence. The rest may well be occupied by galahs. The spacing is related to the foraging requirements of the birds, because they survive by knowing their territory intimately and exploit different sources of food efficiently without undue competition. A 450sq km (280sq mile) area studied by a team of CSIRO scientists based in Perth harboured only 16 pairs of Major Mitchell's cockatoos, while a further 100 birds were forced to stay in a non-breeding flock. By contrast, 350 pairs of galahs were nesting in the area.

Throughout the wheat belt, the survival of six kinds of cockatoos is ultimately linked to the presence of mature salmon-gum and wandoo trees which supply the majority of nesting hollows. Unfortunately, settlers recognised the fact that soils supporting salmon-gums produced the best cereal crops. As a result, very few strands of these trees exist, even inside the established sanctuaries. Blocks of surviving salmon-gums on private land are therefore crucially important to cockatoos prospecting for nests in this pastoral landscape. Competition for vacant hollows is severe as these become scarcer by the year. Galahs and the recently introduced sulphur-crested cockatoos have the competitive edge over other species because the mated pairs maintain an interest in their cavities all year round, so are able to fend off other parrots, tree ducks and possums when they try to commandeer the holes.

Dr Dennis Saunders of CSIRO surveyed a 25ha (62 acre) block of salmon-gums that were left after the surrounding land was cleared for sheep and wheat. There were 173 trees, and these had 241 hollows suitable for breeding cockatoos; during the spring of 1978, 47 per cent were occupied, 48 by galahs, 28 by corellas, 16 by inland red-tailed black and 1 by a short-billed, white-tailed black cockatoo. However, the trees were not regenerating. On the contrary, in successive years he discovered that an increasing proportion of them were becoming unhealthy and dying. Even the wooded areas are being increasingly managed for timber and to feed the insatiable appetite for wood-chippings. If the industry is allowed to carry on without any regard for wildlife interests, the result will be the gradual replacement of mature trees with young ones. The land set aside for forests will not necessarily diminish, but the trees will be unsuitable for parrots to nest in.

One is driven to the conclusion that in this part of Australia, most of the super-parrots are having a difficult time in maintaining their numbers. And yet, to a casual observer, there appear to be plenty of large mobs of cockatoos in agricultural areas. Dr Saunders believes that these are deceptive and belie the true position. Flocks sometimes draw in most of the cockatoos which live over a very large region. They may also consist largely of adults which may not have successfully bred for several years. Being long-lived birds, the lack of recruitment of young birds into the population may not show for several years, until a significant number of adults have died. There is therefore no room for complacency.

Some Australian parrots are in great demand for cage birds. Although none can be legally exported, nests are regularly raided and the birds smuggled out. Major Mitchell's cockatoo is especially threatened by over-collection because of its value in Europe and North America. However, many species throughout the world are endangered by our passion for parrots

OUR LETHAL PASSION FOR PARROTS

A boldly worded sign in the Bird House at the Bronx Zoo, New York, reads:

NEVER BUY A PARROT OR MACAW.
THEY ARE DECLINING EVERYWHERE
THEY BREED SLOWLY AND THEIR CAPTURE OFTEN INVOLVES CASUALTIES.

Unfortunately, vast numbers of people choose to ignore this sound advice, so the very existence of the birds that we adore is being threatened simply to satisfy our passion to own a parrot.

There is no business like bird business, especially if parrots and macaws are involved. Over the past twenty-five years, the trade has been revolutionized by the advent of cheap, fast, air transportation, so that today almost any kind of bird can be sent around the world without too much difficulty. With virtually the whole of the bird kingdom on offer – legally or otherwise – the pet-bird buyers, especially in North America and Japan, have gone for the big, the bright and the gaudy. 'Parrot fever' has brought handsome profits, with huge mark-ups; a fledgling macaw sold for $5 by a Brazilian peasant may fetch $6,000 in a fashionable New York pet shop. Every species has its price tag. In the US, palm cockatoos are in vogue; knocked off their roosting perches in the Aru Islands a month or so before, and transported in cane 'sleeves' via Irian Jaya and Singapore, a pair may cost at least $30,000. A couple of Major Mitchell's cockatoos smuggled out of Australia change hands under the counter in Manhattan for $20,000, whereas $3,000 secures a sulphur-crested polly. Small amazons and African grey parrots fetch between $200 and $1,000, but the flashy macaws are in the expensive league. Macaw mania has driven their value up, while their numbers in the wild sink lower and lower. Spix's macaw has vanished from its native haunts, and Lear's macaw has virtually disappeared from the wild; but the lucrative trade in cage birds is the single most important factor endangering the survival of the rarest macaws and cockatoos, like the salmon-crested from Seram.

The hyacinth macaw, the giant of the parrot world once widespread in parts of Brazil, is now suffering a catastrophic collapse in numbers. A recent survey of its traditional haunts revealed that there may be only 2,500 or so left yet, during 1988, 500 of these exquisite parrots were trapped and illegally exported from Brazil, and many more were probably smuggled out undetected. Like all large parrots, the hyacinth macaw is a slow breeder, and so it cannot sustain a high level of trapping without being seriously depleted. And yet the species is protected!

In theory, all parrots, excepting budgerigars, ring-necked parakeets and cockatiels, are safeguarded against excessive exploitation by the international bird market. Australia has strict laws forbidding the export of its animals and plants, so all parrots from that continent are protected from that kind of abuse. However, since 6 June 1981 the trade in parrots has been regulated by the Convention on International Trade in Endangered Species of Fauna and Flora (CITES). The majority of parrots are placed on Appendix 2, which means that the country from which the birds are shipped must only issue export permits if the consignments do not jeopardize the survival of the species in the wild. Each country ratifying the treaty must keep a tally for each species, and forward these to special monitoring units; the figures are then collated for each kind of parrot, so that warnings can be given if the level of trade becomes excessive. Extremely rare or very threatened species are placed on Appendix 1, which expressly forbids all international trade. In 1987, both the palm cockatoo and the hyacinth macaw were transferred to this category, thus making it illegal to export, let alone import, these fine birds into any country which abides by CITES. Alas, both species are still being offered for sale in the US, the EEC countries and Japan. Wealthy collectors give $10,000 for hyacinth macaws smuggled from Brazil. With the current level of undercover shipments to Spain, Singapore and Hong Kong, the outlook for this gorgeous macaw looks grim. Before too long, the birds may only survive in captivity, like Spix's macaw.

The scale of the trade is quite astonishing. Africa is the largest bird-exporting region in terms of sheer numbers. Senegal is now the world's cheapest source of cage birds. The licensed dealers export 2½ million from Dakar each year, representing a total catch of around 20 million! In 1984, a large part of the business was in parrots. At least 126,000 representing 16 out of the 23 species, were exported from a variety of countries. Fischer's lovebirds, Senegal and African grey parrots dominated the trade. The latter species is one of the most heavily traded parrots in the world because of its remarkable 'talking' ability; in 1984, at least 44,000 entered the market, with perhaps one-third originating in the Cameroons where peasants regard them as pests. However, many were allegedly caught in Mali and Togo where the species is scarce.

Between 1981 and 1984, 20,000 parrots a year entered the United Kingdom, a modest figure compared with the annual inflow into Japan and the US where 100,000 and 225,000 were imported respectively. Nearly 100 countries are involved in the global bird business. The US is the largest consumer because of its size and affluence. According to the US Fish and Wildlife Service, the business is worth $1,000 million a year, of which a quarter is illegal. The statistics make chill reading. During the year ending September 1984, nearly a million birds (913,653) were legally imported. However, TRAFFIC(USA) that monitors international trade in animals and plants, estimates that the real import figure is nearer 4 million. Parrots figure prominently in these imports. Between January 1982 and June 1984, 402,410 neotropical parrots were brought into the USA. They represented at least 96 of the 141 species native to South America. Nearly as many came in again from Africa and Asia. Further trade statistics reveal where the neo-tropical ones may have originated.

Argentina has the dubious distinction of being the heaviest trader of parrots in South America, with over 175,000 shipped out annually. In 1985, 72,000 parrots went to the US alone. The totals for individual species are no less impressive. Over 7,000 Tucuman amazons were exported between 1984 and 1986; the species is now scarce in its native province of Tucuman. Between 1980 and 1984, over 50,000 grey-cheeked parakeets were shipped out of Ecuador and Peru; in the latter country, the bird business was worth $20 million in 1983.

In recent years, Guyana has become one of the major suppliers of parrots for the pet market. Although a system of quotas is in force – amounting to 36,720 birds a year – the figures for individual species are not based upon whether the wild populations can sustain such a harvest. For example, the annual quota for orange-winged amazons has been set at 17,500 birds. It is possible that this common species may be able to take this level of trapping, but it is doubtful whether the blue and yellow macaw can sustain any at all, let alone a quota of 2,400 birds a year. Unfortunately, there is also a thriving illegal trade.

Tens of thousands of parrots are thought to be exiting Mexico and Venezuela annually. Some of them leave by devious routes, because the dealers and their middlemen have devised way of circumventing bothersome export regulations in countries which have ratified CITES. The seriousness of the clandestine trade was revealed recently when it was estimated that as many as 10,000 macaws and other parrots are spirited out of the Orinoco Delta via Trinidad and Guyana. Both scarce species and the popular blue and yellow kind leave Trinidad with documents to 'prove' that the birds were caught locally and, as such, can be legally offered to the international bird trade. However, there are no wild macaws left on the island! They are caught somewhere else in South America and smuggled across the narrow strait which separates Trinidad from Venezuela, whereupon export permits are issued which enable the macaws to enter the US, Japan or Europe without too many questions being asked. Such deplorable ruses are practised all over the world. The European Economic Community has forbidden the import of African grey parrots from Gabon, but these are still entering Europe, having been 'laundered' through Senegal at £54 per bird. During the early 1980s, Bolivia issued export permits for 1,500 hyacinth macaws, despite the fact that its own indigenous population barely amounted to 500.

The parrot business has been nothing if not opportunistic. As one route closes, so another opens. Honduras in Central America increased its market share of parrot exports to the US when the flow of birds from Guatemala decreased. But the shipments from Honduras were mostly of four species of amazons, which doubtless intensified the pressure on the populations of those birds. Among them was a species that does not occur in Honduras. In 1984, 34 red-spectacled amazons were shipped to the United States. In fact, these parrots only occur in a small area thousands of miles away in the south-eastern part of South America. In addition, the species was listed on Appendix 1 of CITES, and so should not have been traded for commercial purposes.

The practice of 'laundering' siphons parrots away from countries where they are supposed to be protected. The US has a law, the Lacey Act, which forbids the importation of species protected in their own countries. This was used to confiscate a shipment of 100 palm cockatoos and 28 eclectus parrots worth $700,000 at Miami airport in 1983. The dealers obtained export permits from Malaysia, but the birds originated in Indonesia. The paperwork was considered to be 'irregular' and so the contraband was seized.

The scarlet macaw was once common in Central America, but is now nearly extinct in that area due wholly to the removal of huge numbers of birds from the forests. However, those that were left behind also suffered after the trappers had left. The parrots were usually intercepted in their roosts, but during the breeding season the hens tend to stay in their nests, so it was the cocks that were caught. These were the birds that provisioned their families so, with the disappearance of the cocks, the hens and their chicks probably perished.

The majority of wild-caught birds embark on a journey to death. Most, if not all, the techniques of capturing wild birds involve an element of cruelty in the first place whether it be netting, liming, trapping, wing tipping (shooting not to kill but to slightly injure flying birds) or plundering nests which is often achieved by cutting down trees simply to steal young parrots. Some are killed by the initial shock of capture. Others, perhaps as many as 25 per cent, succumb to the change of food and, if overcrowding is serious, the mortality rate may double, carpeting the dealer's aviaries with piles of feathered corpses. And the long trail of mortality continues as consignments are shipped all over the world, usually in the pressurised but cold cargo holds of aircraft. In 1986, of the 31,408 wild parrots imported into the UK, 1,451 (4.6 per cent) were dead on arrival and another 4,434 (15 per cent) did not survive their stay in quarantine.

Smuggled birds may have an even harder time, travelling in makeshift, badly ventilated cages, inadequately provided with food and water. In the case of the large parrots, they are often drugged, their bodies bound and their beaks taped shut to stop them squawking. They sometimes pass through customs constrained in socks or tight mesh cylinders, in pockets, suitcases or under the floorboards of small boats; it is a wonder that so many survive the stress of such blatant cruelty. Of course, many do not; it is estimated that, for every bird that reaches the market place, as many as three or four others may have died. This is the hidden cost of the trade in wild birds, and should be unacceptable to civilised people. And yet our plundering of wild parrots continues unabated.

Rich collectors who covet parrots continue to finance illicit dealings in protected species, paying fortunes not only for spectacular birds like palm and Major Mitchell's cockatoos, but also for parrots that are hardly ever seen in captivity. Recently, one of the scarce shining parrots from the Pacific was allegedly on offer in Europe for £25,000. Such rarities sometimes slip through in consignments of more commonly traded species. The importers themselves often complain about the maze of confusing regulations and the sheaves of documents required to transport birds around the world. Indeed, these may be a source of some of the difficulties faced by conservationists, because permits can be fudged – deliberately or otherwise – to conceal the true nature of the cargo and its real place of origin. Many rare and endangered parrots must pass through customs and quarantine under the guise of common species, scrutinized by officials who can barely tell one bird from another, let alone discern the subtle differences between, say, a bunch of amazons.

If caught with illegally imported parrots, many a dealer has offered the excuse that his birds were bred in captivity, even if the specimens were not wearing 'closed rings' that can only be slipped over the clenched foot of a youngster. However, sophisticated science is now coming to the aid of the conservationists. In October 1988, the Alkmaar district court fined a Dutch aviculture firm dfl50,000 (£13,000) for incorrectly claiming that three young hyacinth macaws were the captive-bred offspring of older birds in their possession. To test their claim, the Ministry of Agriculture and Fisheries in the UK was asked to use the technique of genetic fingerprinting developed for forensic scientists, and which has been used to convict rapists and murderers. It involves analysing and comparing the DNA of chromosomes, so that individuals who are very closely related produce results which match better than those who are not. The tests proved conclusively that the three young birds were not related to the adults. The real parents were doubtless still in Brazil.

While the passion for parrots continues, the lethal trade will carry on. Some countries, like Australia, refuse to allow the export of their natural treasures and clamp down heavily upon those who are caught breaking the law. In August 1988 a courier was caught illegally importing macaws into Sydney, and attempting to export a batch of Australian parrots including 23 Major Mitchell's cockatoos and 10 gang-gangs, all secreted in suitcases and worth $240,000. He was sent to languish in jail for three years. Later, in October, an Austrian citizen was sentenced to five years' imprisonment by a Sydney court.

Such is the value of super-parrots that a new crime has evolved – parrot rustling. With the ability to walk away with feathered swag worth £50,000, villains have taken to breaking into private parrot collections and dealers' aviaries, sometimes resorting to violence if caught in the act. The enterprise is as profitable as breaking into a bank without the risk, at least until recently. Now, the owners of valuable macaws and cockatoos are converting their premises into highly secure areas with video systems, floodlights, security guards and dogs. Perhaps the parrot owners should train some of their birds to shriek in alarm at the presence of strange intruders. In New York, it is possible to have pet parrots trained as 'bird alarms'. There is even a high-tech method of foiling criminals. Small radio transmitters can be hidden beneath the skin of valuable parrots and their codes 'read' by special tuners. Should these birds turn up in pet shops or parrot collections, their origin can be easily determined. Doubtless the tightening of the CITES legislation, with more and more parrots being placed on Appendix 1, will curb some of the gross excesses of the trade.

But of one thing we should all be certain, the best place for a wild parrot is in the wild. More people should heed the advice in the Bronx Zoo. Many species are now bred in captivity, and those of us who cannot live without a companionable parrot should turn to these.

Postcript: In October 1989, the ICBP launched its Protect the Parrots campaign aimed at persuading the EEC to ban the import of all parrots at risk – 40 species considered at risk are legally imported – and to evolve strict welfare standards for all parrots in transit.

Over 200,000 parrots are still imported into EEC member states every year, and when trade barriers are lowered in 1992, dealers will be able to move parrots around the Community with ease.

The lesson is clear. Only buy 'captive-bred' birds.

7·PARROTS FOR PLEASURE

People greatly enjoy parrots. But the kind of pleasure they derive from them depends upon where the people come from and their cultural background. Tribesmen, who live in the jungles of the Far East and the Amazon, take great pride in attiring themselves with brilliantly coloured parrot plumage, and some people relish the taste of their flesh. In the western world, we appreciate parrots in several ways; we marvel at their gaudy colours, delight in keeping them in aviaries or are grateful for their company in our houses, according them the status of honorary people, even remembering them in our wills and taking them to court.

PRESTIGIOUS PETS

The tradition of owning a parrot has its origin in ancient times (see Chapter 4). Indeed, until quite recently, the possession of these birds was deemed to be one of the social graces. They were exotic and expensive, and so only the rich and the powerful owned them. The Tudor monarch, Henry VIII, had an African grey parrot which one day fell into the Thames and was rescued only because it called out for a boat! 'Popinjays' decorated royal and papal courts. Later, Charles II who 'never said a foolish thing, nor ever did a wise one', nevertheless set up aviaries of foreign birds in St James's Park, London – evidenced today as Birdcage Walk. He made a gift of a grey parrot to one of his mistresses, the Duchess of Richmond, which she kept for forty years. When she died, a wax figure was made of her and placed in Westminster Abbey. Alas, her pet parrot pined to death shortly afterwards and was laid to rest in the abbey, where it can still be seen today, the oldest stuffed bird in the realm.

BUDGIE APPEAL

Parrots did not become fully accessible to ordinary people until John Gould introduced live budgerigars to Europe in 1840. In fact, these diminutive nomads from central Australia had been known about since the turn of the century. The first specimen to reach England was a bird shot at Rose Hill, Parramatta, New South Wales, in 1804. This was exhibited in Bullock's Museum, London, and was illustrated in Shaw and Nodder's *Naturalist's Miscellany* of 1805 as an undulated parakeet, *Psittacus undulatus*. It was Gould who eventually added *Melo*, meaning song, to its scientific name, thus conferring on the budgerigars the generic name *Melopsittacus* that we know it by today. At the time, several names were in common currency including shell, zebra and warbling-grass parakeets. The first reference to something approaching the modern name of budgerigar, derived from an aboriginal term, appeared in a letter written by William Gardner. He was a settler from Scotland and became employed as a teacher in an area where the little parakeets abounded. Sometime after 1830, he mentioned *budgerry gaan*. Also Benjamin Delessert, a French traveller, in his book entitled *Souvenirs d'un Voyage à Sydney (Nouvelle Hollande) fait pendant l'année 1845* refers to a visit to a Sydney curio shop owned by an ex-convict called John Roach. He was an excellent taxidermist and his premises were a compulsory visiting place for all who were interested in the natural treasures of the island continent. In it, Delessert saw a mounted parakeet, leaf-green in colour with a striped back, called a budgerry. He also noted that it could be taught to talk. The word budgerigar in its modern spelling was not coined until 1870 in *Cassell's Household Guide*.

When these little seed-eating parakeets with beguiling 'baby-faces' were brought to Europe alive, they were a sensation. Luckily, they bred easily and prodigiously in captivity to supplement the demand for imports. One dealer had 79,655 pairs shipped into London in 1879. Is it to be wondered that the Australian government prohibited all exports in 1894? By then, budgies were breeding all over the world. The first recorded nesting in Europe was in Paris, in 1846, although four years later Antwerp Zoo was producing them in numbers. Such was the developing craze for these cute little parrots that 'budgie farms' were established, initially in the south of France; the largest owned by M Bastide was at Toulouse and housed 20,000 breeding birds which produced 10,000 young a year. By 1913, it had expanded to 100,000 budgies and covered a hectare (2 acres). The budgerigar was also taken to the hearts of the German people. In 1880, about 10,000 birds were reared by commercial breeders and fanciers, escalating to 25,000 ten years later. By the end of the century, tens of thousands of these puny parakeets had been sent to Russia, South Africa, South America and the USA.

The appeal of budgerigars was further enhanced by the appearance of birds with different colour schemes. At first only wild-type green birds were available. However, in 1872 the first yellow or lutinos were raised in Brussels, followed by startling blue birds in 1878. White budgerigars did not appear until 1921. Since then, the application of genetic principle by fanciers has led to a whole spectrum of varieties such as greys, opalines, cinnamons, clear-winged, yellow-faced sky blue, rainbows and even crested birds.

Today, the budgerigar is by far the most numerous parrot in the world; in Great Britain alone, there are reckoned to be 5 million. The species was almost designed for captivity. Budgies are small and hardy, being intensely gregarious, couples obligingly nest in serried ranks of nest boxes without needing large territories. They also require little else other than a good supply of millet supplemented by vitamins, grit and water to keep them healthy.

Despite their intensely sociable nature, it is the fate of huge numbers of budgerigars to live alone in ornamental cages in our homes. These are fundamentally unfulfilled creatures. However, a whole industry has evolved to lessen the loneliness of the single budgie, producing mirrors, spring-loaded toys and shiny bells which reflect and respond to the bird's billing, thus partly making up for the absence of companions. Ladders and swings challenge the inmate's climbing ability, and clip-on baths provide welcome 'water holes'. But such is the need for others that, like most lone parrots, they adopt their human owners and respond to them as though they were birds. This is, of course, exactly what makes them so rewarding as pets. So often, the human guardians are looking for companionship on undemanding terms; what could be better than a friendly, baby-faced parrot that talks.

WHO'S A CLEVER BIRDIE?

It is the parrot's apparent mastery of language which makes it so appealing, and confers upon it a human quality to which even our closest cousins – the monkeys and apes – cannot aspire. With an ability to converse, joke, answer back, curse and blaspheme, parrots transcend the role of being just decorative. To many people, a parrot is an agreeable companion, an amusing friend, or simply someone to swear at.

The first budgerigar in Europe recorded as speaking did so in the German tongue. It belonged to Fräulein E. Maier of Stuttgart. In 1877, her avian companion entreated her to give it a kiss! Nowadays, every person who owns a budgerigar expects it to talk as well as squawk. But in many birds, the powers of oratory go well beyond reciting 'Pretty boy. Give us a kiss'. Great Britain's champion chatterbox was the famous Sparkie Williams, who talked himself into the *Guinness Book of Records* in 1958 by winning the BBC's Cage Word contest. The competition was severe, with 3,000 entries including Skippy, a sulphur-crested cockatoo who always laughed at his own jokes, and Percy, an unstoppable mynah who had needed elocution

An archive photograph of Mrs Mattie Williams' talking prize-winning budgerigar Sparkie from 'Language of Birds' by Jeffery Boswall, Proc Roy Inst, 1983

lessons to change his broad Geordie accent. Many got stage fright and were tongue-tied when it was their turn to address the judges, but not Sparkie. He put on a virtuoso performance, reciting eight, four-line nursery rhymes flawlessly without drawing a breath. Hailed as the bird world's greatest spokesman, this launched him on a lucrative career as a budgie star. He travelled 24,000km (15,000 miles) with his mistress, Mrs Mattie Williams of Bournemouth, starring in TV commercials for bird seed, and being a VIB (bird) guest on radio and TV chat shows.

Sparkie was also signed up by a record company and cut a single-play disc explaining the best method of teaching birds to talk. By the end of his busy life, he had a vocabulary of 531 words, and had committed to memory 383 sentences. On 4 December 1962 he uttered his last words, 'Love you Mama', whereupon he fell from his perch, aged eight. Such was his status, that *The Times* carried an obituary, and a ten-minute tribute to this remarkable talking green budgerigar was broadcast on BBC radio's 'Woman's Hour'.

Birds like Sparkie possess a formidable repertoire but are they really talking? Sometimes they lapse into a confusing babble of sound, and their sentences become scrambled; but they have their lucid moments when they perform fluently. Mrs Williams maintained that her parrot prodigy did not utter the first thing that came into his head because he never said a single word out of place. People who keep talking parrots are nothing if not loyal. Without a doubt, a speaking bird will use the right words in the correct context because it has been taught that way. Someone who keeps a parrot in a cage is likely to greet it with 'Hullo' on entering the room, and to wish it 'Goodnight' before turning the lights out. Any feather-brained parrot will learn to associate these salutations with the behaviour of its owner, and give them in the correct context. No great intellectual power need be invoked to account for this kind of performance. However, human language involves the creative use of words and grammar, often to express abstract concepts. Thoughts are also intimately connected with language; but what kind of thoughts can exist without a vocabulary? Many scientists believe that talking birds are simply good mimics, and have no idea what they are saying. Their talking is no more than a refined form of squawking. However, Irene Pepperberg, an ethologist at Purdue University, West Lafayette, Indiana, has conducted research which suggests that parrots may be cleverer than we think.

Pepperberg's star pupil was a grey parrot called Alex, purchased in a Chicago pet store when it was just over a year old. The grey parrot was a good choice for this kind of investigation because the species mimics

Irene Pepperberg's grey parrot Alex (Kevin Horan)

expertly and talks clearly, although its diction is not quite as good as that of the Indian mynah. Alex was chosen to help the scientist reveal whether parrots could use words to identify objects and ask for them. Ultimately, Pepperberg hoped to discover if these birds had the talent to rearrange words in different ways to make fresh sentences and to embrace simple concepts like colour, shape and size.

When Alex was bought, he was speechless and could converse only in a medley of high-pitched screams and shrill whistles. Before his tutorials started, Pepperberg researched how parrots learn in the wild. Like many birds, parrots are not born fluent in their own tongues, but need to perfect their language by listening to and imitating their own parents. Whereas the majority of small song birds pass through a very brief period, usually when they are in the nest, during which time they absorb the details of vocalisation, parrots have a learning phase which seems to persist potentially for life. Curiously, they do not seem to exercise their talent for mimicking in the wild like starlings, although some populations of parrots appear to develop local dialects. Only in captivity do their imitative powers seem to flourish to the full. Bereft of other con-specifics to converse with, they turn their ear to all manner of sounds from dripping taps, telephone bells, falling bombs to human speech. No formal lessons are required.

Pepperberg's technique was to let Alex see her instructing someone else. This method was first tried by a German ethologist, Dietmar Todt, who soon found that his parrot used to capture his attention by butting in and uttering new sentences. Pepperberg reinforced Alex's understanding of words by offering him what he asked for, and not by rewarding him with food. If he specifically asked for a nut, he would be given one. If he said 'cork', he would receive a cork to play with. Alex was quick to learn the names or 'labels' of objects that commanded his attention, like shiny keys or pieces of wood that he could chew or scratch himself with. By comparison with a human child, he was slow to learn, but well up to the standard of parrot pupils. After twenty-six months of speech training, Alex acquired a working vocabulary which

Hawk-headed parrot raising its fan-like crest (Francisco Erize/Bruce Coleman Ltd)

MACROCERCUS ARACANGA.

Red and Yellow Macaw.

2/5 Nat. Size.

enabled him and his human companions to converse. He could utter the names of nine 'things' such as paper, key, wood and peg wood (wooden clothes-peg); he 'understood' three colours – rose (red), green and blue. He had also mastered phrases to indicate shape and could use the word 'no' correctly.

By careful testing, Pepperberg demonstrated that Alex had a way with words, and displayed a glimmer of the mental abilities which were once thought to be peculiar to ourselves. When shown objects like a piece of paper or a walnut, Alex nearly always correctly identified them. He also perceived quantities up to six. But there was more. As his vocabulary expanded, he learned to make requests, using the word 'want'. He would sometimes interrupt an experiment by saying 'want banana' and would resolutely refuse to cooperate until his trainers gave in. He apparently mastered the use of abstract words like 'same' and 'different'. For example, when he was shown a green wooden square and a red wooden square, and asked 'what's the difference?', Alex would reply, 'colour', even if he had not seen the objects before. Some of the exchanges took on the nature of a conversation. On one occasion, Alex asked his trainer to tickle his head – ie to social groom him, and, as the trainer leaned forward, the parrot fixed her with its beady eye and said 'gentle'!

Irene Pepperberg insists that she is not being duped by an artful parrot, nor is she observing language deployed in the sophisticated way in which we use it. However, if her interpretation of what she is seeing is correct, the large parrots do seem to be able to use a few words in the correct context and to represent some simple but abstract concepts verbally. And yet, strict comparison with our own performance is difficult to make because a bird's brain is very different from our own. It does not possess a greatly expanded cerebral cortex which is the centre of our intelligence and vocal learning. 'Clever' birds like parrots, jays, crows and mynahs use a part of the brain called the hyperstriatum. Whatever thoughts flit through their minds – and few

Edward Lear's 'Red and Yellow Macaw' from his Illustrations of the Family Psittacidae, or Parrots (Linnean Society/Weidenfeld & Nicolson Archives)

Top talkers and mimics

Grey Parrot

Budgerigar

Starling

Hill Mynah

Marsh Warbler

Raven

Mockingbird

scientists today doubt that animals do think – have very different neural origins to our own.

This raises the whole question of parrot brain-power. These birds have a reputation for being intelligent, but is it justified? Intelligence is a slightly nebulous concept, but in practical terms means an ability to weigh up situations and take the appropriate actions. A chimpanzee has no trouble in placing some boxes, one on top of the other, to reach a banana placed beyond its reach. By trial and error, by copying, or by sheer insight, clever creatures tend to modify their behaviour to fit the circumstances rather than meet situations with a series of rigid 'instinctive' responses. The behavioural repertoire of most animals includes a combination of both learning and instinct although some depend more upon one than the other.

We tend to infer intelligence in creatures like dolphins, higher primates and parrots which display manipulative and cognitive skills. Parrots certainly give the impression of being wise birds that realise what is going on around them. There are several reasons why they appear clever. They possess inquisitive natures, examining and 'handling' objects like we do. Parrots are also very gregarious and so a lone one tends to focus its attention onto its human owner and be very reactive to company. Lastly, their astonishing ability to mimic the human voice and apparently to engage in conversation seals the parrot's reputation as an avian intellect.

All this does not mean that every parrot is a pure genius except for surviving in a particular way in the tropics. Nevertheless, flexibility, opportunism and a talent for handling things are qualities that we also exploited during the course of our evolution and so, in a sense, we recognise parrots as kindred spirits. But this does not make them superior birds. Pigeons, for instance, have done very well as a family with 255 species found throughout the world and yet no one would rate doves for their sagacity.

COMPUTING PARROTS

There is good experimental evidence that parrots and birds like jackdaws and ravens, can recognise numbers. The technique used to reveal their counting ability was to train them to take food from one particular bowl among a group of bowls according to the number of black spots on the lid. First, the birds were shown a mastercard with a number of spots, and they then had to select the bowl displaying the same number of spots. Of course, there are a great many bird circuses which feature mathematical parrots, but these are invariably tricks that the birds have been trained to perform *en cue*. Proving that birds have a concept of numbers takes careful experimental design.

In the scientific tests, the shape of the spots and the patterns were varied so that there was no chance that the parrots could simply match the pattern on the mastercard with that on one of the bowls. These experiments showed that parrots seemed to be able to grasp the idea of numbers up to seven. However, all attempts to teach birds simple mathematics have failed.

PROSECUTED PARROTS

Pet parrots' voices sometimes cause trouble with the people next door. In the central Brazilian state capital of Belo Horizonte, a football-crazy parrot was taken to court for keeping the neighbours awake at night with sleep shattering shrieks of 'Goal!'. The bird was duly served with an eviction order which was staunchly contested by the owners. Despite a month-long hearing, the law was upheld and the vociferous parrot had to go.

Rico, a German parrot which barked, was more lucky when he was taken to court. He had learned to imitate with great accuracy the incessant yapping of the neighbour's dog. Unfortunately, the dog's owners did not appreciate the parrot's barkings so they took the bird and its keeper to the Lüneburger District Court, confident that settlement would be made in their favour. Luckily, the judge was well briefed in the ways of parrots and expressed the opinion that the bird's perfor-mance did not exceed the local ambient noise level. Furthermore, the bedlam was created by the hound who, by his persistent barking, had stimulated the parrot to imitate him in the first place.

A few years ago, an Israeli parrot was summoned to court to give evidence. Headlined in the press as 'Polly Puts the Cackle On', it was alleged that she was stolen from a home in Haifa, although the current owner vigorously disputed the charge. However, the original owner reckoned that the dispute could be settled if the parrot could be made to sing and recite before a magistrate nursery rhymes that he had taught it. Alas, the performance was inconclusive.

LONG-LIVED PARROTS

One of the reasons why large parrots make particularly satisfying companions is that they have potential life spans approaching our own three score years and ten. Cocky Bennett was supposed to have been 120 years old when he died in 1916. He was a sulphur-crested cockatoo owned by Mrs Sarah Bennett, proprietor of the Sea Breeze Hotel at Tom Ugley's Point near Sydney, Australia. This talking parrot became something of a celebrity, and doubtless many of the stories of his prowess with words are apocryphal. Towards the end of his life, this geriatric cockatoo became almost naked and he was often heard to cackle 'One more fucking feather, and I'll fly', much to the merriment of the hotel guests. However, his claim to have lived virtually since the days of the First Fleet might not have been justified. Cocky was only in the care of Mrs Bennett for his final twenty-six years. She acquired him from an old sea salt, Captain George Ellis, skipper of a South Seas' sailing ship who claimed that the bird was alive when he was serving an apprenticeship at the age of nine. But was it really Cocky Bennett?

This illustrates the difficulty in assessing the veracity of such claims. They often depend upon a history that cannot be easily confirmed. Certainly, there is no shortage of records of century-old birds in parrot literature. In 1968, another sulphur-crested cockatoo died in Nottingham Park Aviary 'aged 114'. However, several cockatoos answering to the name of Cocky were housed in this aviary over the years. One year later, the death was announced of yet another Cocky at Bridge Sollers in Herefordshire, reputedly aged 125. But the bird's plumage was in suspiciously good condition when the cockatoo met its demise, indicating that it was considerably younger; super-parrots begin to look decidedly tatty when they reach 40 to 50 years of age.

Parrots certainly live a long time in captivity if they are well cared for. The smaller species have shorter lifespans than their larger relatives. A budgerigar can expect to reach 8, but is doing well to survive its twelfth birthday. The Veterinary Institute of the University of London has a record of one called Peter which lived for 17 years, 111 days. When this was published in the German magazine *Das Tiere*, a reader reported that his own pet budgie had been in the family for 22 years. Many of the medium-sized parrots seem to be capable of enjoying life for between 20 and 40 years. A peach-fronted conure survived for 21 years in the family of a German ornithologist, Karl Neunzig, and a tame Senegal parrot lived in captivity in Switzerland from 1924 until 1960, thus reaching at least 36 years of age. The records of the London Zoo reveal that a vasa parrot spent 54 years, and a blue and yellow macaw 64 years, in the Parrot House. A healthy grey parrot can easily reach 50 years, and a few cosseted cockatoos and macaws can probably survive for 70 or more. In 1968, the death of a grey parrot was reported, allegedly 99 years old. Unfortunately, there were so many unsubstantiated gaps in the bird's history that the bird's true age remains in doubt. The real Methuselah of the parrot world seems to be Müller's parrot which is a large green species from the Philippine and Celebes islands. One was apparently kept for 81 years in the von Spiegel family in Halberstadt in Germany, and there is another reliable account of one surviving for 85 years.

Of course, in the wild, parrots never live as long as their captive cousins which are protected from disease, predators and the stresses and strains of everyday life. The majority of young parrots fail to attain breeding age, and even adults can be cut down in the prime of life. Five years might be a good life expectation for a wild budgerigar, whereas a corella or sulphur-crested cockatoo might be fortunate to reach over 20 years.

THE FATAL ATTRACTION

Since being a pet can so prolong a parrot's life, it is ironic that there is a small chance that it will drastically shorten the life of its owners. This is the down-side of our pleasure in keeping these long-lived birds. In the beginning, parrots were thought to be harmless; but in 1879 a mysterious malady broke out in Switzerland. Dr Jacob Ritter was called to the house of a parrot enthusiast and discovered seven members of the family very ill indeed; three were already beyond his ministrations and were dying. All were running a high fever and suffering from severe inflammation of the lungs. What could be the cause of this dangerous condition? Dr Ritter's suspicion was aroused by the presence of a dying parrot bought three weeks earlier by the master of the house. Parrots had already been suspect in both France and Germany where their presence had been correlated with a new illness which bore a resemblance to both typhus and pneumonia. Dr Ritter's patients showed that 'parrot fever' had now reached Switzerland. Another small epidemic broke out in Paris in 1892 affecting 42 people, 14 of whom died. Professor Peter Michael studied the outbreak, and was in no doubt that diseased parrots, many of which had recently been imported from Argentina, were to blame. It was Antonine Morange, another French doctor, who in 1895 called the lethal complaint psittacosis, thus giving force to the suspicion that parrots could kill.

It is now known that psittacosis is caused by one of a class of pathogens called *Chlamydia* carried by birds. They share certain properties with both viruses and bacteria. Like viruses they live inside the cells of their hosts, and like bacteria they can be destroyed by some antibiotics. *Chlamydia* occur in many species of birds, being active chiefly in juveniles which catch the disease from their parents while they are in the nest. Infection causes the young birds to become lethargic, their eyes become inflamed, their noses discharge and they suffer from diarrhoea. Those that survive recover without long-lasting effects, but carry the pathogens for the rest of their lives. Parrots carry a particularly virulent form called *Chlamydia psittaci.* Since parrots and people often come into close contact with each other, the opportunities for cross-infection are relatively high.

An infection usually starts with a sick parrot. Simply handling or being bitten by the bird is sometimes enough to start the disease, but people normally contract 'parrot fever' by inhaling feather fragments or dust from dried droppings. Those in contact with many infected birds, like dealers or aviculturists, are particularly at risk. After an in-cubation period of between one and two weeks, symptoms similar to influenza appear, with headache, limb and back pains. A week later, a fever develops, the spleen swells, and pneumonia sets in. For most people, the high temperature subsides after a few days and slow recov-ery ensues. But for the elderly, the outlook is less good. They are hit hardest by the lung inflammation and the other debilitating effects of the disease.

One of the largest epidemics took place in 1929-30, and seemed to confirm the theory that South America was the source of psittacosis. In 1929, large numbers of parrots, chiefly amazons, that were being held in Argentina showed signs of ill-health. Many of these ailing birds were shipped abroad and caused outbreaks of 'parrot fever' in three continents. By the following spring, 825 cases had been notified; 150 were in Argentina, 215 in Germany, 196 in North America and 125 in Great Britain. For 143 of them, their passion for parrots proved fatal.

The notion has been put forward that some of the consignment of 5,000 sick parrots sent to Europe may have been responsible for infect-ing the fulmars of the Faeroes with the lethal *Chlamydia*. A few of the birds reached Denmark, and from here some may have been shipped northwards. Those that died of psittacosis may have been thrown overboard between the Hebrides and the Faeroes, and the carcases consumed by fulmars nesting on the Faeroes. If so, this might explain the presence of the *Chlamydia* in the fulmar chicks which caused an-nual outbreaks in humans between 1933 and 1937. Out of 165 cases, 24 people succumbed to the illness. The islanders' appetite for young fulmars was their downfall, because psittacosis was always contracted in September, mostly by women who had been employed splitting and salting the catch. The epidemics led to immediate government legis-lation outlawing the harvesting of fulmars for food.

There was also a clampdown for health reasons on the easy impor-tation of wild parrots into many countries. In 1934, Germany issued a decree prohibiting imports, causing the trade to continue with captive-bred birds. Elsewhere, strict quarantine regulations were enforced. The risk of contagious psittacosis was by no means eliminated,

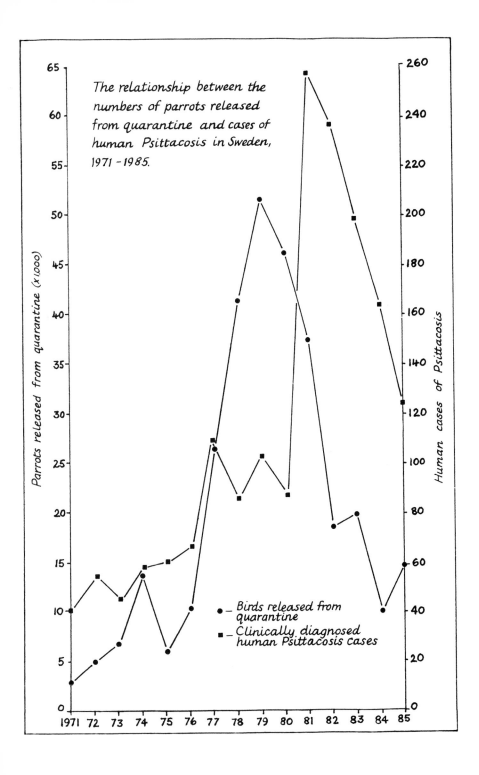

The relationship between the numbers of parrots released from quarantine and cases of human Psittacosis in Sweden, 1971 – 1985.

Parrots released from quarantine (x 1,000)

Human cases of Psittacosis

● — Birds released from quarantine

■ — Clinically diagnosed human Psittacosis cases

1971 72 73 74 75 76 77 78 79 80 81 82 83 84 85

because *Chlamydia* was already established in captive stock, and wild parrots were still being traded illicitly.

Further scientific research revealed that South American parrots may have been too hastily accused of originating the disease. The original infection probably came from Australia. In the 1930s, a batch of wild-caught budgerigars was examined and a large proportion of them were found to be carrying the dreaded pathogens. Positive results were also obtained from other Australian cockatoos, lories and parakeets. Most of the individuals were robust adults and displayed no ill-effects of hosting the *Chlamydia,* but there is evidence that the disease manifests itself when birds become distressed for some reason or other. This happened in January 1939 near Adelaide, when large numbers of rosellas dropped dead from the trees, stricken with psittacosis. Epidemics of ill and dying king parrots were also recorded in Victoria, and rosellas were struck down in Tasmania. It seems likely that psittacosis is endemic to Australian parrots and that the causative agents were ferried around the world, probably in budgerigars.

Today, powerful antibiotics such as erythromycin have taken the lethal sting out of 'parrot fever', providing the condition can be diagnosed in time. Nevertheless, it is still possible to become 'as sick as a parrot'. Indeed, there is a fear that the disease is on the increase, fuelled by the trade in both legal and smuggled birds. Official British government statistics show the prevalence of the disease in highly stressed imported parrots. In 1986, of the 31,408 wild parrots that entered the UK chiefly through Heathrow airport, 1,451 were dead on arrival. A further 4,160 (13 per cent) died in quarantine of psittacosis and other lethal conditions; a further 274 were put down.

There is still a very small risk of contracting psittacosis wherever people come into contact with wild parrots or captive stock contaminated with the virulent *Chlamydia.* In England, at the time of writing, the disease is more common than tuberculosis, but is a notifiable disease only in Cambridgeshire where there are between three and four cases a week in a population of about one million. In four years, four fatalities were reported. However, the medical authorities have a lurking suspicion that over the whole country dozens of people, especially elderly ones with 'pneumonia', have in fact been killed by their pet birds. The lesson is clear. All trade should be in captive-bred birds which can be given a guaranteed clean bill of health.

PARROTS FOR THE POT

There is an Australian recipe for cooking cockatoos. You take a galah and fling it into a pan with an old boot. After thoroughly boiling them for a couple of hours, you throw away the galah and eat into the boot. This sums up our disdain for eating these birds. But is parrot meat that bad?

In the western world, we are clearly not partial to parrot flesh, and yet our menus regularly include offal of all kinds and such curious items as snails, frog's legs and cheese – putrefied cream. Even in Chinese restaurants where shark's fin and bird's nest soups are served, you will not find any dish based upon parrot. However, tribal people have no compunction in eating these birds, and many a traveller has found cooked parrot infinitely more digestible than shoe leather.

The aboriginal inhabitants of Australia hunted parrots of all kinds. Indeed, the derivation of 'budgerigar' clearly reflects the natives' interest in the birds as food. Handfuls of these small parakeets, caught with fine nets or by hurling sticks into dense flocks around water holes, were placed on the embers of fires to singe the feathers, and the birds were then consumed virtually whole. Cockatoos were also killed with boomerangs. The first European settlers were not impressed by their bitter taste. However, John Gould compared the meat of the ground parrot with that of snipe, being tender and juicy.

The Mascarene Islands were looted for their edible birds by seafarers who were doubtless so thankful for anything fresh that their powers of gustatory discrimination were considerably blunted. However, the French colonist, François Lequat, greatly esteemed the young of Newton's parakeet, reckoning that they were as good as young pigeons.

In Africa, reports vary as to the quality of grey parrot flesh. Some commented that it was delicious, others rated it little better than galah. Apparently, the flavour of the flesh varied according to the birds' diet. If they had been gorging themselves on bitter seeds, the meat was unpleasantly sharp; but if they had been feasting on cashew nuts, the flesh was fragrant. On the Guinea coast, parrots feeding on the slightly fermented seed of 'cotton trees' enter a drunken stupor, whereupon they fall into the clutches of the native people, presumably already marinated.

Parrots have been relished in South America for as long as people have inhabited the continent. Columbus confirmed that the natives of the Caribbean islands consumed both amazons and macaws. The latter were thought to taste rather like tough beef, but this did not diminish the demand for them served up as food. The amazons were generally pot-roasted, and the young were 'like little lumps of fat and similar to partridge'. A particularly popular dish was made out of parrot tongues, echoing a meal that was enjoyed in Rome 1,500 years previously. The tribal people of South America are still keen on young parrots. In 1982 Martin Maissner, a German teacher, reported that amazons were hunted in the forests around the Rio Xingu by the Kamayura Indians, and the meat could pass for home-roasted chicken, pheasant or partridge.

Parrots are killed for the pot in Papua New Guinea. In the western highlands, people hunt the birds with nets and special bird arrows. They make clearings in the forest for their settlements, but leave a couple of mature trees in the centre which lure the birds to perch and rest. Platforms are erected in the crowns where the armed hunters can sit and await the arrival of the parrots, many of which are slaughtered by the deadly arrows. For many tribal people that live in remote parts of that island, the consumption of parrots is governed by strict regulations. Large birds can be eaten only by initiated and married men; smaller species are reserved for the boys; women are allowed to ingest only certain kinds of parrots and so on. Parrot eggs are reserved only for women and girls. Such is the complexity of the rules relating to the tribal allocation of foods, that parrots deemed fit to eat by one clan may be taboo to another. Apparently people would rather starve to death than break these bans. Parrot flesh is sometimes more than mere nourishment.

Pygmy parrots, plucked, wrapped in leaves and roasted over an open fire are still considered to be a good cure for stomach pains. In the Middle Ages, Conrad Gesner stated that parrots possessed curative properties for 'all kinds of jaundice and devastation of the lungs'. In those days, the preparation was probably expensive and totally ineffective.

The people of Papua New Guinea have yet another interest in catching parrots – for their lavishly coloured feathers.

PARROTS FOR DECORATION

People the world over have always looked enviously at the colourful feathers and plumes of birds. Our own bodies are rather dull, so we have supplemented what nature has given us in all kinds of ways. In the tropics this urge to decorate the human form has often led to parrots being divested of their plumage.

Columbus was greeted in the Caribbean by people wearing bunches of parrot feathers. The Aztec ruler, Montezuma II, stocked a vast birdhouse in his capital, Tenochtitlan, which contained examples of every kind of pretty bird that he could secure in that part of the world. According to Hernando Cortez, the Spanish conqueror of Mexico, the aviaries served, among other things, to provide a ready supply of colourful parrot feathers in which there was a lively trade. Antonio Pigafetta, the chronicler of Magellan's expedition of 1519-22, wrote that the Indians of east Brazil wore nothing except loin-cloths incorporating long parrot feathers which covered their posteriors in a very amusing way. Macaw feathers were greatly prized by the Incas of Peru, who made imposing head-dresses out of them. Then as now, the tribal people of Amazonia decorated themselves with brilliant red, blue and yellow feathers, usually from macaws, often fixed to head-bands from which they radiate in a spectacular fashion. The Alban Indians even pierced their cheeks and ear lobes with feathers, wearing them like jewellery.

The Amer-Indians obtained their feathers from birds which they had hunted down, or from pets. Some kept parrots primarily for plucking, and developed techniques to make the birds grow the red and yellow feathers that were most valuable of all. Young birds were taken from their nests, the new plumage torn from their backs, and their skin massaged with the blood of a particular kind of noxious frog. Only a few fledglings survived this drastic treatment, but those that lived grew the prized red and yellow feathers instead of green ones. Unfortunately for the traumatised parrots, they were once more robbed of their beautiful but aberrant plumage and again rubbed with frog's blood. Alfred Russel Wallace, the distinguished Victorian naturalist who rivalled Charles Darwin in his ideas about evolution, saw parrots being fed on the fat of a large Amazonian catfish, causing the fresh feathers to be gloriously flecked with red and yellow. Even today, the technique of doctoring the food of tame macaws is used by Amer-Indians; furthermore, the red- or yellow-inducing fat is rubbed into the skin of birds during their moulting period so that fresh feathers take on a deeper and more satisfying hue.

Parrot plumage, especially if crimson, was much sought after in the Pacific. In the Society Islands, warriors used to wear bunches of small scarlet parrot feathers which were considered as valuable as diamonds were in Europe. The Maori chiefs in New Zealand wore capes made out of the soft green plumage of kakapo, and the reddish-orange under-wing feathers of the kaka were deployed like decorative jewellery.

In the matter of body decoration, the tribal people of New Guinea are unquestionably the most colourful in the world. They literally transform their swarthy frames into ravishing works of art by using body paints and wearing plumes of every conceivable shape and colour. At tribal ceremonies, the men wear dazzling head-dresses which sway and shimmer, mostly with the plumage of birds of paradise. However, as second best, the feathers of other birds are also used, including those of owls, egrets and chickens. The red, yellow and green feathers of parrots occasionally dominate the creations and, in head-dresses worn by men from the Mount Hagen region, complete skins of Papuan lories are arranged with their long, yellow-tipped tails pointed vertically to look like the points of a crown. For less ostentatious occasions, a single bird is sometimes slung around the neck and hangs like a medallion on the chest. Women occasionally wear parrot wings around their waists for decoration. The crimson-red belly plumage and secondary wing feathers of Pesquet's parrot are especially prized by the Wahgi-speaking people who obtain them from tribes in the central mountainous areas in exchange for coffee; brides may even be bought for the payment, in part at least, of these sumptuously coloured articles.

PARROTS ON PARADE

Brightly coloured parrots are excellent showbirds. Nowhere is this truer than in Florida's Parrot Jungle. Situated just south of Miami in an area of native woodland, it is possible to witness a variety of super-parrots put through their paces. In a sense, parrots are natural clowns. They look comical, waddle and can be trained to use their feet and beaks to carry and manipulate objects when given the correct cues. Under the roof of the Parrot Bowl stadium, a succession of free-flying cockatoos, macaws and parrots display their virtuosity by raising the Stars and Stripes, playing games with toys, 'counting', roller skating to music, and riding bicycles on a tight-rope. This parrot circus happens six times daily and usually before a packed and adulatory audience, It does not tell you much about parrots apart from revealing their potential as trained avian clowns.

There is another parrot show in the Canary Isles. Situated at Loro Parque in Tenerife, it is a major tourist attraction. Here, parrots per-form on trapezes, play basketball and ascend in balloons. Free-flying birds add interest to the sub-tropical gardens, and a film screened in Loro Vision depicts the 'mad world of man as seen through the eyes of a parrot'. However, Loro Parque has a serious side because it has over 230 kinds of parrots and boasts the largest collection in the world. It is therefore a Mecca for parrot enthusiasts and managed by Rosemary Low who is one of the greatest authorities on these birds. The centre is also engaged in research which might be applied to the preservation of some rare species.

In England, there are places where parrots are paraded in more trad-itional ways. The peace and quiet of Bourton-on-the-Water, a quaint old English village located in the Cotswolds, is periodically shattered by grating screeches of macaws and cockatoos as they swoop over the roof tops. These birds come from Birdland. Originally established by Len Hill, a local builder who had a passion for penguins and parrots,

The Perpendicular Purple Polly,
who read the Newspaper and ate Parsnip Pie
with his Spectacles.

this avian zoo has a good collection of captive species; a few free-flying macaws, including a hyacinth, add to the attraction. Free-flying macaws can also be seen near the Georgian city of Bath where Donald and Betty Risdon established their Tropical Bird Garden in the elegant grounds of a country house. For parrot enthusiasts these are, however, fairly modest collections compared with the Walsrode Vogelpark, near Hanover, Germany.

Walsrode Bird Park is situated in beautifully managed parkland with expanses of lawn with fountains, clusters of fir trees, colourful flower beds and aviaries galore. A million people every year visit this privately funded bird menagerie, including parrot lovers from all over the world. A thousand kinds of birds are kept in the heated tropical houses and aviaries, many of which are large enough to walk through. However, the gaudy and noisy parrots dominate the attention with 200 species on show. Walsrode is not merely a 'stamp' collection of living parrots. Much research takes place behind the scenes into the problems of keeping and breeding parrots in captivity, and some of the data is being applied to the conservation of rare amazons and lories. There are forty secluded breeding enclosures for the courting couples, and their progress is monitored through minute peep-holes. The Bird Park also finances two overseas operations based in Majorca and the Dominican Republic, where the climate is rather more conducive to breeding endangered tropical parrots.

Australia offers the most spectacular parrot parade in the world, all the more impressive because the birds are wild. It is at Currumbin, south of Brisbane on Queensland's Gold Coast, an area of extravagant development in the pursuit of sun and fun. A part of Currumbin Sanctuary operates like a mighty bird-table. The stars are thousands of flower-feeding lorikeets – chiefly dazzling rainbows – that are bribed to drop in by copious handouts of ersatz nectar. This is offered to them in a small oval arena with two contraptions which resemble on a miniature scale the 'big wheels' of fairgrounds and which are fitted with perches and plate-holders. Early in the morning and late in the afternoon, keepers dish out a mixture of honey and soggy bread, and some of the plates are given to visitors to hold while others are placed on the rotating wheels. The hungry lorikeets descend from the gum trees in their thousands in a welter of whirring wings, causing the wheels to spin. They flutter onto the arms, shoulders and heads of those in the crowd who are proffering food. It is a delightful and exciting show which never fails except when the local eucalypts are in blossom. At this time, the lorikeets prefer the natural nectar and pollen. It is a satisfying sight that only goes to show that, given the right formula, wild parrots and people can live very happily together to mutual benefit.

Cockatooca Superba

(Edward Lear)

THE LAST WORD

My first encounter with a parrot was with a green budgerigar called Billy belonging to my sister. Perhaps it was his persistent chattering that originally aroused my interest in these birds. Since then, I have been lucky enough to have travelled the world both as a Producer and as Head of the BBC's Natural History Unit. During these trips I managed to observe parrots and to meet many scientists, ornithologists and film makers who generously shared their knowledge and experiences. They are too many to name individually. However, I am particularly indebted to Donald Trounson who allowed me to use some of his original research into the origin of Mercator's Psitacorum Regio; Jim Frazier and Densey Kline whose enthusiasm for Australian parrots was very infectious; John Young, an extraordinarily skilled bush-naturalist in whose company I spent many fascinating hours in northern Queensland; Dr Hans Strunden who sent me a translation of some of his fascinating research on the involvement of parrots in our culture; Dr Pat Rich of Monash University who put me in touch with the field of fossil parrots; Wincey Willis who revealed the world of the parrot collectors; and Tricia Dewing who speedily and with great precision translated foreign texts.

This book represents a pulling together of information from numerous sources – scientific papers, newspaper articles, official documents and other texts. Needless to say, if I have failed to do justice to them, the fault is mine.

Parrots, A Natural History has had a long gestation period. It was originally conceived in 1970 with my friend Tony Soper as the last of a trilogy on 'pop' birds. *Penguins* and *Owls* are still going strong after twenty years; this title took a little longer. I am duly grateful to my publisher, David St John Thomas, for his patience, and to Pam

Griffiths whose gentle advice in the editing of this book was much appreciated. It also gives me great pleasure to record my thanks to Robert Gillmor whose skilled illustrations embellish the pages of this and the other two books in the series.

Lastly, my wife Sara had to endure a three-month period when my thoughts were single-mindedly on parrots. She took the loneliness out of the word processing by her cheerful presence and encouragement.

THE PARROTS
OF THE WORLD

(AFTER FORSHAW & COOPER 1973). In November 1989 the third, revised, edition of this book was published, with 340 species (including extinct ones) described and a new system of classification.

* Indicates that bird is on the ICBP World Checklist of Threatened Birds
† Indicates sub-species

PARROTS OF THE PACIFIC DISTRIBUTION

Loriidae		Vini	(Kuhl's Lory)*
Chalcopsitta	Black Lory		Henderson Lorikeet (Stephen's Lory)*
	Duyvenbode's Lory		Blue (Tahitian) Lorikeet (Lory)*
	Yellow-streaked Lory		Ultramarine Lorikeet (Lory)*
	Cardinal Lory	Glossopsitta	Musk Lorikeet
Eos	Biak Red (black-winged) Lory*		Little Lorikeet
	Violet-necked Lory		Purple-crowned Lorikeet
	Blue-streaked Lory*	Charmosyna	Palm Lorikeet
	Red and blue Lory*		Red-chinned Lorikeet
	Red Lory		Meek's Lorikeet
	Blue-eared Lory		Blue-fronted Lorikeet*
Pseudeos	Dusky Lory		Striated Lorikeet
Trichoglossus	Ornate Lory		Wilhelmina's Lorikeet
	Rainbow Lory		Red-spotted Lorikeet
	Ponapé Lory		Red-flanked Lorikeet
	Johnstone's Lorikeet		New Caledonian Lorikeet*
	Yellow and Green Lorikeet		Red-throated Lorikeet
	Scaly-breasted Lorikeet		Duchess Lorikeet
	Perfect Lorikeet		Fairy Lorikeet
	Varied Lorikeet		Josephine's Lory
	Iris Lorikeet		Papuan Lory
	Goldie's Lorikeet	Oreopsittacus	Whiskered Lorikeet-
Lorius	Purple-bellied Lory	Neopsittacus	Musschenbroek's Lorikeet
	Black-capped Lory		Emerald Lorikeet
	White-naped Lory		
	Stresemann's Lory	Cacatuidae	
	Yellow-bibbed Lory	Cacatuinae	
	Purple-naped Lory*	Probosciger	Palm Cockatoo
	Blue-thighed Lory	Calyptorhynchus	Black Cockatoo
	Chattering Lory		Red-tailed Cockatoo
Phigys	Collared Lory		Glossy Cockatoo
Vini	Blue-crowned Lory	Callocephalon	Gang-gang Cockatoo
	Scarlet-breasted Lorikeet	Eolophus	Galah

Cacatua   Major Mitchell's Cockatoo
Yellow-crested (Lesser Sulphur-
   crested) Cockatoo *
Sulphur-crested Cockatoo
Blue-eyed Cockatoo
Salmon-crested Cockatoo *
White Cockatoo *
Red-vented Cockatoo *
Tanimbar (Goffin's) Cockatoo *
Little Corella
Long-billed Corella
Ducorps' Cockatoo

Nymphicinae
Nymphicus   Cockatiel

Psittacidae
Nestorinae
Nestor   Kea
Kaka
Norfolk Island Kaka

Micropsittinae
Micropsitta   Buff-faced Pygmy Parrot
Yellow-capped Pygmy Parrot
Geelvink Pygmy Parrot
Finsch's Pygmy Parrot
Red-breasted Pygmy Parrot

Psittacinae
Opopsitta   Orange-breasted Fig Parrot
Double-eyed Fig Parrot
Psittaculirostris   Desmarest's Fig Parrot
Edwards' Fig Parrot
Salvadori's Fig Parrot *
Bolbopsittacus   Guaiabero
Psittinus   Blue-rumped Parrot
Psittacella   Brehm's Parrot
Painted Parrot
Modest Parrot
Madarasz's Parrot
Geoffroyus   Red-cheeked Parrot
Blue-collared Parrot
Singing Parrot
Prioniturus   Green-headed Racket-tailed Parrot *
Blue-crowned Racket-tailed Parrot
Mountain Racket-tailed Parrot
Red-spotted Racket-tailed Parrot
Golden-mantled Racket-tailed Parrot
Buru Racket-tailed Parrot *
Tanygnathus   Great-billed Parrot
Blue-naped Parrot
Müller's Parrot

Tanygnathus   Rufous-tailed Parrot
Black-lored Parrot
Eclectus   Eclectus Parrot
Psittrichas   Pesquet's Parrot
Prosopeia   Red Shining Parrot
Masked Shining Parrot
Alisterus   Australian King Parrot
Green-winged King Parrot
Amboina King Parrot
Aprosmictus   Red-winged Parrot
Timor Red-winged Parrot
Polytelis   Superb Parrot
Regent Parrot
Princess (Alexandra's) Parrot
Purpureicephalus   Red-capped Parrot
Barnardius   Mallee Ringneck Parrot
Port Lincoln Parrot
Platycercus   Green Rosella
Crimson Rosella
Yellow Rosella
Adelaide Rosella
Eastern Rosella
Pale-headed Rosella
Northern Rosella
Western Rosella
Psephotus   Red-rumped Parrot
Mulga Parrot
Blue-Bonnet
Golden-shouldered Parrot *
Hooded Parrot * †
Paradise Parrot *
Cyanoramphus   Antipodes Green Parakeet *
Red-fronted Parakeet
Yellow-fronted Parakeet
Orange-fronted Parakeet
Black-fronted Parakeet
Society Parakeet
Eunymphicus   Horned Parakeet
Neophema   Bourke's Parrot
Blue-winged Parrot
Elegant Parrot
Rock Parrot
Orange-bellied Parrot *
Turquoise Parrot
Scarlet-chested Parrot *
Lathamus   Swift Parrot
Melopsittacus   Budgerigar
Pezoporus   Ground Parrot *
Geopsittacus   Night Parrot *
Strigopinac
Strigops   Kakapo *

The Parrots of the World

231

The Parrots of the World

Conuropsis Carolina Parakeet
Cyanoliseus Patagonian Conure
Pyrrhura Blue-chested Parakeet
  (Blue-throated Conure)*
Blaze-winged Conure
Maroon-bellied Conure
Pearly Parakeet (Conure)*
Crimson-bellied Conure
Green-cheeked Conure
Yellow-sided Parakeet (Conure)*
White-eared Conure
Painted Conure
Santa Marta Conure
Fiery-shouldered Conure
Maroon-tailed Parakeet
El Oro Parakeet
Black-capped Conure
White-necked Parakeet (Conure)*
Flame-winged Parakeet
  (Brown-breasted Conure)*
Red-eared Conure
Rose-crowned Conure
Hoffman's Conure
Enicognathus Austral Conure
Slender-billed Conure
Myiopsitta Monk Parakeet
Bolborhynchus Sierra Parakeet
Mountain Parakeet
Barred Parakeet
Andean Parakeet
Rufous-fronted Parakeet*
Forpus Mexican Parrotlet
Green-rumped Parrotlet
Blue-winged Parrotlet
Spectacled Parrotlet
Sclater's Parrotlet
Pacific Parrotlet
Yellow-faced Parrotlet
Brotogeris Plain Parakeet
Canary-winged Parakeet
Grey-cheeked Parakeet*
Orange-chinned Parakeet
Cobalt-winged Parakeet
Golden-winged Parakeet
Tui Parakeet
Nannopsittaca Tepui Parrotlet
Touit Seven-coloured Parrotlet
Scarlet-shouldered Parrotlet
Red-winged Parrotlet
Sapphire-rumped Parrotlet
Brown-backed Parrotlet*
Golden-tailed Parrotlet*

Spot-winged Parrotlet*
Pionites Black-headed Caique
White-bellied Caique
Pionopsitta Pileated Parrot
Brown-hooded Parrot
Rose-faced Parrot
Barraband's Parrot
Saffron-headed Parrot
Caica Parrot
Gypopsitta Vulturine Parrot
Hapalopsittaca Black-winged Parrot
Rusty-faced Parrot*
Graydidascalus Short-tailed Parrot
Pionus Blue-headed Parrot
Red-billed Parrot
Scaly-headed Parrot
Plum-crowned Parrot
White-headed Parrot
White-capped Parrot
Bronze-winged Parrot
Dusky Parrot
Amazona Yellow-billed Amazon
Cuban Amazon
Hispaniolan Amazon
White-fronted Amazon
Yellow-lored Amazon
Black-billed Amazon
Puerto Rican Amazon*
Tucuman Amazon
Red-spectacled Amazon*
Red-crowned (Green-cheeked)
  Amazon*
Lilac-crowned Amazon
Red-lored Amazon
Red-tailed Amazon*
Blue-cheeked Amazon
Red-browed Amazon*†
Festive Amazon
Yellow-faced Amazon*
Yellow-shouldered Amazon*
Blue-fronted Amazon
Yellow-crowned Amazon
Orange-winged Amazon
Scaly-naped Amazon
Mealy Amazon
Vinaceous Amazon*
St Lucia Amazon*
Red-necked Amazon*
St Vincent Amazon*
Imperial Amazon*
Deroptyus Hawk-headed Parrot
Triclaria Purple-bellied Parrot*

232

FURTHER READING

Many books and scientific papers have been consulted during the writing of this book, and they are too numerous to itemise in full. It is possible to fill a library with avicultural literature alone. The following list is a guide for those whose appetite has been whetted; it is by no means exhaustive.

Brockway, B. F. 'Ethological studies of the budgerigar: reproductive behaviour', *Behaviour*, 23 (1964), 294-324

Carter, N. and Currey, D. *The Trade in Live Wildlife*. 2nd report by the Environmental Investigation Agency (1987)

Cemminck, D. and Veitch, D. *Kakapo Country* (Hodder & Stoughton, 1987)

Collar, N. J. and Andrew, P. *Birds to Watch*. ICBP Technical Publication No 8 (1988)

Dilger, W. C. 'The comparative ethology of the African parrot genus *Agapornis*', *Z. Tierpsychol*, 17 (1960), 649-85

Finney, C. M. *To Sail Beyond the Sunset. A Natural History of Australia, 1699-1829* (Rigby, 1984)

Ford, H. A. and Paton, D. C. (Eds) *The Dynamic Partnership: Birds and Plants in Southern Australia*. The Flora and Fauna of South Australia Handbooks Committee and D. J. Woolman, Government Printer (1986)

Forshaw, J. M. and Cooper, W. T. *Parrots of the World* 3rd revised edition (Blandford Press 1989). This is a sumptuously illustrated classic; the first edition published by Lansdown is a collector's piece. There is a further volume entitled *Australian Parrots* by the same authors published by Merchurst in 1988.

Fuller, E. *Extinct Birds* (Viking/Rainbird, 1987)

Harrison, C. J. O. 'Allopreening as agonistic behaviour', *Behaviour*, 24 (1965), 161-209

Hindwood, K. A. 'The nesting of birds in the nests of social insects', *Emu*, 59 (1959), 1-37

Hyman, S. *Edward Lear's Birds* (Weidenfeld & Nicolson, 1980)

Keast, A., Recher, H. F., Ford, H. A. and Saunders, D. *Birds of Eucalypt Forest and Woodland* (RAOU and Surrey Beatty & Sons, 1988)

Le Gay Brereton, J. and Immelmann, K. 'Head-scratching in the Psittaciformes', *Ibis*, 104 (1962), 169-74

Long, J. L. *Introduced Birds of the World* (A. H. and A. W. Reed, Sydney, 1981)

Low, R. *Lories and Lorikeets* (Paul Elek, 1977)

Low, R. *Endangered Parrots* (Blandford, 1984)

Meredith, C. W. *The Ground Parrot*. RAOU Conservation Statement No 1 (1984).

Morris, D. 'The feather postures of birds and the problem of the origin of social signals', *Behaviour*, 9 (1956), 75-113

Mountfort, G. *Rare Birds of the World* (Collins, 1988)

Noske, S. 'Aspects of the Behaviour and Ecology of the White Cockatoo (*Cacatua galerita*) and Galah (*C. roseicapilla*) in croplands in north-east New South Wales', MSc Thesis, University of New England, Armidale, NSW (1980). Available from the RAOU on microfiche

Pasquier, R. (Ed). *Conservation of New World Parrots*. ICBP Technical Publication No 1 (1981)

Pepperberg, I. M. 'Functional Vocalizations by an African Grey Parrot (*Psittacus erithacus*)', Z. Tierpsychol, 55 (1981), 139-60

Perry, D. *Life above the Jungle Floor* (Simon Schuster, 1984)

Rowley, I. *Bird Life* (Collins, Sydney, 1975)

Saunders, D. A. 'The breeding behaviour and biology of the short-billed form of the white-tailed black cockatoo *Calyptorhynchus funereus*', *Ibis*, 124 (1982), 422-55

Scoble, J. *The Complete Book of Budgerigars* (Lansdowne Press, 1981)

Serpell, J. A. 'Factors influencing fighting and threat in the parrot genus *Trichoglossus*', *Animal Behaviour*, 30 (1982), 1,244-1,251

Sibley, C. G., Ahlquist, J. E. and Monroe, B. L. 'A classification of the living birds of the world based on DNA-DNA hybridization studies', *Auk*, 105 (1988), 409-43

Trounson, D. and Trounson, M. *Australia, Land of Birds* (Collins, Sydney, 1988)

Wood, G. A. 'Tool use by the palm cockatoo *Probosciger aterrimus* during display', *Corolla*, 8 (1984), 94-5

Wyndham, E. 'Ecology of the Budgerigar *Melopsittacus undulatus* (Shaw) (Psittaciformes: Platycercidae)' PhD Thesis, University of New England, Armidale. NSW (1983). Available from the RAOU on microfiche

In Germany, a number of excellent books for parrot enthusiasts are published by Horst Müller Verlag, Walsrode including:

Arndt, T. *Papageien – ihr Leben in Freiheit*

Enzyklopadie der Papageien und Sittiche (11 vol)

Strunden, H. *Papageien einst und jetzt.* This is a fascinating compendium about the involvement of parrots in human culture.

In Australia, it is possible to purchase for A$294 a set of 7 video cassettes called *Land of Parrots*, produced by Grant Foster with Joseph Forshaw as consultant. They include some visually arresting material, including a sequence of palm cockatoos using a stick to drum on a hollow branch. Obtainable from: Documentaries of Australasia, PO Box 206, Turramurra, NSW 2074

In the UK the Parrot Society produces a monthly magazine, obtainable from 19A De Parys Avenue, Bedford, England.

INDEX

Index